MUSHROOM MAGIC

Michael Jordan
gained his passion for the world of fungi
whilst studying for his biology degrees at University.
Over the years he has spent much time wandering the autumn woodlands
collecting and identifying. His work in television commands most of his time
and he travels extensively, but when the occasion permits he leads
forays of mushroom enthusiasts and is a keen photographer.
He lives in the heart of rural Somerset, in a converted church,
with his wife Diane, children James and Victoria,
and a family dog, Joe.

MICHAEL JORDAN

Mushroom Magic

ELM TREE BOOKS · LONDON
in association with
Channel Four Television Company Limited

ACKNOWLEDGEMENTS

Thanks to:
British Mycological Society; David Chambers; Chesswood Produce Limited;
Darlington Mushroom Laboratories; Forestry Commission; Elena Giandio;
Professor D. Hawksworth, International Mycological Institute;
Mushroom Growers Association; National Poisons Information Service;
National Trust, Witley Common; Sara Shepley;
Seale Hayne Agricultural College; Audrey Thomas; Professor John Webster.

The television programmes on which this book is based
were produced for Channel Four Television
by Bamboo Film & Television Productions Ltd.

All photographs by the author except
frontispiece; p. 86 (all three photos); 87; 94; 95; 102; 103,
courtesy of Bamboo Film & Television Productions Ltd.

ELM TREE BOOKS

Published by the Penguin Group
27 Wrights Lane, London W8 5TZ, England
Viking Penguin Inc, 40 West 23rd Street, New York, New York 10010, U.S.A.
Penguin Books Australia Ltd, Ringwood, Victoria, Australia
Penguin Books Canada Ltd, 2801 John Street, Markham, Ontario, Canada L3R 1B4
Penguin Books (N.Z.) Ltd, 182–190 Wairau Road, Auckland 10, New Zealand

Penguin Books Ltd, Registered Offices: Harmondsworth, Middlesex, England

First published in Great Britain 1989 by
Elm Tree Books
Copyright © 1989 by Michael Jordan
57910864

Book design by Trevor and Jacqui Vincent

Line drawings by A. D. Henry

British Library Cataloguing in Publication Data
CIP data for this book is available from the British Library

ISBN 0–241–12862–5
0–241–12844–7 pbk

Typeset by Wyvern Typesetting Ltd
Made and printed in Great Britain by
Richard Clay Ltd, Bungay, Suffolk

Frontispiece] Haldon Forest, near Exeter –
superb country for fungus forays!

CONTENTS

Lepista nuda

1
Fruiting Bodies

My voice
Becomes the wind;
Mushroom-hunting.

19TH CENTURY HAIKU BY THE JAPANESE POET SHIKU

Not far from Guildford in Surrey, there is an old bridle track along the side of which has been dumped a large amount of earth. Where the soil came from nobody seems certain, but it holds the germ of a unique and in its way, quite beautiful plant.

By late July this year, about a dozen specimens were approaching their full-blown glory. There they sat in tranquil splendour beside the path where people exercise their dogs and take their summer picnics, until one morning someone came along and smashed them so thoroughly into oblivion, that it was difficult to appreciate that they had ever grown there.

Had these been rare summer flowers, there would have been outraged letters in the local press, and conservation groups would have demanded action. Sadly for the victims, they enjoyed no such protective mystique. They were only the 'flowers' of *Langermannia gigantea*, so the incident passed by with no more than a murmur of indignation from the enlightened few who had savoured the prospect of taking the ripened beauties home for tea! To most Britons, the Giant Puff Ball is, after all, a bizarre and faintly disgusting freak of nature.

If similar vandalism had happened in France, there would have been a different reaction: the threat of a trip to the Bastille would have hung over the offenders. In Italy, days of mourning might have ensued. In Czechoslovakia, heaven knows what could have happened to the culprits!

On the Continent, they view fungi with the same level of reverence that we keep for an orchid, a wild rose or the first crocus of spring. Why, from a very early age, we in Britain should be instilled with such a phobia about fungi is not clear. Most townspeople will merrily plunge into country hedgerows and strip them of blackberries. A surprising number extol the delights of sloes, hazelnuts and rosehips, but about fungi we are illogically and stubbornly reserved. Such aberrations of nature are still taboo to all but very few of us.

Yet they are not only some of the most fascinating plants on earth, they are, in the main, surprisingly benign forms of life. In the British Isles, there are about 3500 species of mushrooms and toadstools big enough to pick, examine with the naked eye, sniff and savour. Very few of them will do us any harm.

The distinction between 'mushroom' and 'toadstool' is one of the first anomalies to dispense with because, in fact, there is no scientific distinction. It is about as valid as the nuance which divides 'flower' and 'weed'. An arbitrary line has traditionally been drawn to separate the specimens currently in vogue for commercial growing and eating from all other wild fungi.

The vogue has tended to change with the times. In the midland shires not so many years ago, they sold 'blewits' (*Lepista nuda*) as 'mushrooms'. These days most people seeing a blewit on a supermarket shelf would categorise it as a toadstool, and eye it most dubiously as a contender for position on their breakfast plate. So what are mushrooms and toadstools?

They are not, as most people might think, whole plants consisting of a cap on a stalk with a bit of straggly root attached. The objects which appear on woodland floors and out of the trunks of trees are the very loose equivalent of a flower on a garden plant. Just as a flower is an intricate piece of natural design, with the sole purpose of nursing and liberating ripe seed, so mushrooms and toadstools are the 'flowers' of the fungi. They are factories producing and setting free countless millions of spores. The rest of the fungus, the counterpart of the stem, leaves and roots, consists of a fragile cotton-wool-like mass of colourless threads, spreading in what looks to be a haphazard sprawl through the soil, or into the tissues of another 'host' plant. 'Flower' is an inappropriate term, because there are quite significant differences between the two. That which is the object of desire on the fungus hunt is described as a fruiting body, or sporophore.

[8]

'Mushroom' and 'toadstool' are lay terms for one form of fungus – a stalk with a cap – but there are many other kinds of fungal growth, for which there is no other word than 'fungus'.

Fungi follow a lifestyle that is quite different from that of almost any other form of plant, so they are not bound by the same rules of survival. They use no sunlight to synthesise their food, so they do not need leaves, the light-collecting organs of green plants. For the same reason, none of them need to be grass green. Hence, colours range from garish reds and purples to the most delicate pastel shades of amethyst and pink.

Textures, too, are a constant surprise and delight. They range from the glistening surfaces on the caps of the Porcelain Fungus (*Oudemansiella mucida*), magically translucent in the sunlight, to the scaliness of the Shaggy Ink Cap (*Coprinus comatus*), the velvety stems of Velvet Shank (*Flammulina velutipes*), or the smooth, almost silky sheen of the Death Cap (*Amanita phalloides*).

Nor do they seem bound by the conventions of shape that limit other plant growths. So long as the objective is achieved and their spores are released, the fruiting bodies seem to have been granted total artistic licence, an 'anything goes' dispensation regarding size and shape. Fungi can claim some of the most bizarre constructions on earth. They can emulate anything from a football to a poached egg, a bird's nest and even a remarkably life-like brain. The great majority of fungi use the breeze to carry their spores and the priority is to lift the spore-bearing surface high enough above ground level.

When it comes to spore dispersal by other means, however, there are some interesting surprises in store. One fungus which you are bound to come across sooner rather than later, guided by its smell, has developed such a remarkably risqué shape that Charles Darwin's daughter took urgent steps against it. So appalled was she that such prurient objects lurked in the shrubbery, putting the innocence of questing household maids at risk, that she burned any she found. Editors of the more respectable Victorian journals printed pictures of the specimen, the Stinkhorn (*Phallus impudicus*), upside-down so as not to shock the sensitivities of their readership.

Part of the delight of fungi lies in the enormous range of size. There await to

Oudemansiella mucida

Flammulina velutipes

be discovered, on the one hand, tiny grassland forms so fragile that they last for a single day and even to pick them without damage requires great care; whilst at the other end of the scale are huge, leathery brackets which gradually destroy full-grown trees.

So when and where does one start to look for fungi?

There is a peak autumn season, particularly for 'mushrooms' and 'toad-stools', as distinct from some of the other forms. The season varies from country to country, and shifts considerably even within the British Isles. It tends to be several weeks earlier in the Scottish Highlands than on the South Coast. Generally though, the season runs from sometime towards the end of August to late November depending upon several factors, all of which can influence not only the timing but also the quality. Ideally, a spell of warm wet weather is needed in late July or during August, followed by an autumn which is neither too dry or too cold. Good humid conditions, in other words a fairly typical British autumn, will result in a 'flush' of many of the larger forms within about two or three weeks from the onset of rain.

If the rainfall is sparse or the autumn turns into an Indian summer, then few of the grassland and open forest species will appear, and what does emerge will be limited to damp, shady areas of woodland. Generally the fungi which grow on trees are less influenced by dry weather, and I look particularly for specimens on trunks and stumps on my first sortie of the year. Sometimes when there is a very dry autumn, almost no 'flush' will emerge, but during November there will be a desultory appearance of a few smaller and frost-resistant forms.

A limited number of mushrooms and toadstools produce fruiting bodies all the year round, and some of the more resistant 'brackets' can also be found perennially. There is also a smaller flush, mostly of Cup Fungi and Morels, in the spring months. Few mushrooms and toadstools appear in spring, though the vernal species include the famous St George's Mushroom (*Tricholoma gambosum*) and a few unpleasant members of the Inocybe group. There are also certain non-conformists, including some of the Boletus group and in particular the Giant Puff Ball (*Langermannia gigantea*) which take their bow in high summer.

As to where to find fungi, the answer is practically everywhere! I ticked off more than a dozen species growing in my lawn this autumn, including the Fairy Ring (*Marasmius oreades*). There is a species of Ink Cap, *Coprinus atramentarius*, which regularly sprouts through ashphalt drives where there have been old wooden gate posts. If you possess an elder tree, then it may well keep company with the Jew's Ear Fungus (*Auricularia auricula-judae*).

In other words, you do not have to go very far before you come across specimens, nor do you have to live in the country. City parks and gardens sport generous populations of fungi.

The bulk of species grow in woods and forests, though, because the conditions of humidity and rotting vegetation are ideal. A conifer wood will support different forms from those which grow under broad-leaved trees. This can be an important point of distinction. Two species of Russula, *R. mairei* and *R. emetica*, look confusingly alike, but the one prefers beech woodlands, the other conifers.

Open grasslands and lawns produce their own individual crops, among them some of the tiniest and most delicate. Some fungi will only grow on dung, others are peculiar to rotting sawdust. There are fungi on fungi, including one called *Asterophora parasitica*; fungi that will grow on bricks and mortar; fungi on plastic; and then of course there is a specimen called *Serpula lacrymans*, the Dry Rot . . .

Many fungi are also selectively fussy about the kind of soil they grow on. Some relish the alkalinity of chalk, but dislike acid soils. Others are practically restricted to sand dunes, or sphagnum bogs.

So, autumn has arrived in all its glory! I can think of few more delightful ways of spending a fine Sunday afternoon than wending a lazy path through mellow woodlands, searching for mushrooms and toadstools.

You can either join an organised foray, usually run by the local Natural History or Mycological Society, or you can go it alone. Some of the people who run these outings are terrific. Audrey Thomas regularly leads fungus hunts near her home in Surrey. She is a mine of fascinating tit-bits of information and knows her stuff, yet puts it across in a very unpretentious fashion. There are many like her. If you tag along with an organised group, be

[13]

Inonotus hispidus growing on the side of an ash tree

[14]

Top] Marasmius oreades –
the 'Fairy Ring'

Bottom] Asterophora parasitica

prepared for the chance of a bit of elitist hype, however! There are those who take perverse delight in trying to confound you with jargon and in doing overly-impressive business with much sniffing and spitting. Forget it. The point about fungus hunting is that it is supposed to be fun. All you need to get you going is a good guide book, a sharp eye and a sense of humour. You may also find that carrying a trug or basket is useful if you want to take specimens home to identify them or perhaps to sketch them.

You will often find the greatest selections in old mixed forests. A modern coppiced woodland or plantation will tend to yield less of a range of specimens. Bear in mind also, that in a dry autumn, westerly facing uplands will be damper than lowland woods. I have found plenty to keep me happy in high west-of-England forests, on a clay base and facing the Atlantic, whilst, in the same week, in low-lying woods in Surrey with well-drained sandy soil, I have found next to nothing. The most important thing to do when off on a fungus hunt, is to 'get your eye in'. It is like searching for anything else: once you have the patterns you want to locate fixed in your brain, you start to see them! If there is a problem it is that the patterns are so varied.

3500 species to get to grips with are bound to be confusing for anyone setting off into the enchanting world of mycology.

There are, however, some quite easy guidelines for distinguishing the most important groups, and once you have mastered these, you are well on the way to acquiring a sound knowledge of who is who. There is a listing of all the major groups of Higher Fungi, with their general characteristics, at the back of this book. What do you look for, though, when an unknown specimen is sitting there, daring you to get its name wrong?

The larger fungi are separated into two overall groups, the Ascomycetes and Basidiomycetes. This distinction is based ultimately on features which are only visible under the microscope, the organs which form and liberate the spores. Ascomycetes tend to have very individual appearances and are therefore easier to tell apart. The larger ones include the Cup Fungi, Morels, Truffles and an assortment of odds and ends; some of these are extremely common, notably the Candle Snuff Fungus (*Xylaria hypoxylon*) and the Cramp Ball (*Daldinia concentrica*).

The Basidiomycetes are the main group of fungi which you are likely to be hunting, and there are four main divisions, the brackets (Aphyllophorales); mushrooms and toadstools (Agaricales); earth balls, puff balls, and earth stars (Gasteromycetales), and jelly fungi (Tremellales). All but the agarics tend to be quite individualistic in appearance and are not too difficult to get to know. Agarics are more tricky because of the sheer numbers of them, and in some cases because distinctions between one and another are finely shaded. Agarics are distinguished, in the first instance, by the colour of their spores which in turn tend to shade the gills. Hence, most of the field guides will put all those with white or cream coloured spores together, and will similarly 'lump' rust coloured, salmon pink, clay brown and chocolate coloured spores into separate sections.

For most people who have been wandering the woods and fields identifying fungi for years, it is impossible to recognise all and sundry, so don't try and certainly don't be embarrassed by what seems to be a personal lack of knowledge. We are all, to a greater or lesser extent, in the same boat. What you can do is learn to spot the characteristics of the main families, and then gently build up your repertoire of individuals. Some, like the Amethyst Agaric (*Laccaria amethystina*), or the Parasol Mushroom (*Lepiota procera*), or the Fly Agaric (*Amanita muscaria*), are surprisingly easy – once seen, never forgotten. Others, like some of the obscure Cortinarius and Tricholoma species take an awful lot of time and experience and are generally better left to the specialists to sort out.

When the blackberry pickers or the sloe gin distillers sortie to the countryside after their quarry, they are guided by several factors, which follow not only instinctive common sense, but also good botanical practice. They steer towards places where such species are likely to grow. That observation may seem banal, but it is an important eliminator for many possible look-alikes. They then select their prize having considered texture, shape, colour and perhaps taste and smell. Thus, for the most part, elder berries are not muddled with those of the purging buckthorn, and the sloe gin is spared the inclusion of deadly nightshade fruit. The same principles apply to recognising fungi.

Laccaria laccata var. amethystina

Top] *Xylaria hypoxylon*   [19]

Bottom] *Geastrum triplex –*
one of the earth stars

Watch closely how any experienced fungus hunter behaves once his eye has latched on a new specimen. It may be growing on soil, or on wood which is not always obvious because it may be buried beneath the surface. The first priority is to check if the specimen is growing near a particular kind of tree, since many fungi favour one or another.

Some are very specific in their requirements. Sometimes two species, which seem identical in appearance, can only readily be separated in this way. For instance, *Russula emetica* and *Russula mairei* might well be twins: same size and shape, same pillar-box red caps, same smell and taste. The distinction from the viewpoint of the mushroom-hunter, as I have mentioned, is that the two are separated by the kinds of woodland in which they are able to grow.

Overall build allows instant 'pigeon-holing' into the biggest groupings of fungi. Brackets, agarics, puff balls, jelly fungi and so on, all possess quite obvious gross features. Within the agarics, there are obvious points which will permit narrowing down possible options. The presence of a ring on the stem is an important one, though it needs to be remembered that sometimes these rings can be lost with age. Also, the shape and structure of the base of the stem can be very significant, for which reason it is vital, when trying to identify a specimen, to dig up the whole stem and not merely to break it off at ground level. The lower end may be pointed or bulbous, and the bulb can have a ridge running around the upper margin, or even the remains of a second veil forming a sheathing bag, the volva.

The surface of the cap can say a lot about the identity of a specimen. The Amanita group is usually (though alas not inevitably) characterised by broken patches on the cap. The Lepiota group typically bear shaggy scales.

Many of the members of the Ink Cap group (Coprinus) spread their spores by dissolving the tissues of the cap in a process called autodigestion, which results in an inky fluid, hence 'Ink Cap'. This is another useful identification trait.

Colours which are important for distinguishing between species will be evident at a glance, although experience will teach you that shades can change considerably throughout the life of a fruiting body, and according to the weather. The Butter Cap (*Collybia butyracea*), which looks darkish brown in the wet, can dry to a pale tan or even ivory. Shape of caps will also be self-evident and is sometimes a useful pointer, though again cap shape can vary according to the age of the specimen and the state of the weather. The famous Chanterelle (*Cantharellus cibarius*), for example, starts life with a dome-shaped cap which later turns into a funnel.

Textures are sounder guidelines. Caps which are confusingly similar in colour may sometimes be easily told apart because one is dry and velvety whilst the other is slimy. A tough, woody stem may be a useful signpost, as may be the presence of scales, fibrils, patches or a dusted look. Break a piece of stem to establish if it is fibrous or crumbly. The book of words may list this as an important diagnostic feature.

The hunter who knows what he is about will make a mental note of all these points. The process becomes instinctive, rather like riding a bike. He will then cast a careful eye at several less obvious features.

One of the most important for field identification is the appearance of the 'business' that lies underneath the cap. There are essentially three major design possibilities: gills, which are vertical plates arranged like bicycle wheel spokes; pores; and in a limited number of instances, structures which may at first glance seem like gills but which are in fact more bluntly finished ridges.

Colour of gills is very significant, because one of the bases of identifying agarics is according to their spore tint. Again, though, it is important to remember that spore colour may not develop fully until the cap is mature, and may change still more when the spores ripen. Thus, whilst the members of the dangerous Amanita group always possess white gills, the Agaricus species, to which the common mushroom belongs, have gills that begin a pale salmon or pink and become progressively darker brown with age. As a general principle, it is risky to try to identify a specimen which is either very young or very old. It is better to look around and see if another is growing close by in a more identifiable state.

Shape is equally tell-tale. Gills are described in the field guides according to their profile, which includes the way they join with the stem of the fruiting body. This can often narrow the search for identity. The Tricholoma family, for instance, offers an assortment of colours in gills, but all are sinuate in

Lactarius camphoratus

Tremellodon gelatinosum – a jelly fu

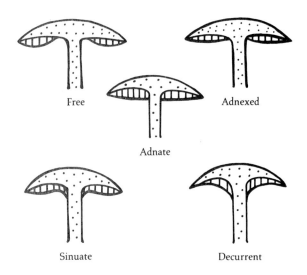

GILL AND PORE ATTACHMENTS IN AGARICS

outline, joining the stem with an S-shaped undulation. On the other hand, the Clitocybe family, another rather loose rambling group, mostly have decurrent gills which have a straight outline that runs at an angle down the stem.

Gill texture and proximity needs to be looked at, too. The Hygrocybe and Hygrophorus families are distinguished by gills with a thick, waxy feel. Sometimes the spacing of one gill from another is a valuable clue. Two of the 'milk caps', *Lactarius piperatus* and *L. vellereus*, are quite confusing at a glance, but the gills of *L. vellereus* are wide apart whilst those of *L. piperatus* are crowded together. On that score, incidentally, it is always worth breaking the gills slightly, because if they produce a milky fluid in any fleshy specimen, it can be immediately and confidently consigned to the Lactarius family.

When all of these points have been checked out, there are still finer details. Many fungi have distinctive odours and flavours. The Curry Milk Cap, *Lactarius camphoratus*, which can otherwise look confusingly like several other small brown specimens, can infuse a whole woodland with the smell of curry. Others smell distinctly of anything from pears to mouse droppings!

Tasting is not recommended for the raw recruit, but the experts will frequently engage in elaborate sniffing, nibbling and spitting before passing their judgement on finer points of identification.

The taste of a particular specimen may often provide valuable clues to its identity, and if the right technique is followed even the most poisonous species can be sampled with safety, though the really poisonous fungi should be recognisable from their more general appearances. A very tiny piece should be chewed between the front teeth and on the tip of the tongue. Spit all the remains out, and clear the mouth thoroughly.

The 'professional' hunter will also sometimes carry an array of chemicals, which for the dedicated mycologist can separate species impossible to distinguish by simpler means. Finally, if all else fails in the field, the spores can be separated from the cap to a microscope slide and inspected.

Much of this more detailed investigation is only of value to the purist, though. A good basic know-how can be built up on the simple distinctions. Certainly most of the notoriously poisonous specimens are quite easy to recognise, and with a bit of practice enough deliciously edible kinds to keep the average gourmet happy can be collected with confidence.

There has to be a word of sensible caution however. Nobody with any sense of responsibility would recommend an Eskimo or someone from the Australian outback to go out and eat berries from an English hedgerow armed only with the experience of pictures in a book. By the same token, there is potential risk for the would-be fungus hunter collecting specimens for eating, without having first been introduced to the good and the bad by one who knows the essential distinctions.

Mere handling of fungi which turn out to be poisonous varieties is harmless. I have dug up lethal fungi with my fingers and waggled them for television cameras, and I am still here to tell the tale. Mind you, I would resist the temptation to lick my fingers, or eat a round of sandwiches until I had washed my hands!

Do not be put off by the terminology which is invariably employed in field guides. People often ask why fungi cannot be called by common names, in the way that flowering plants are generally known. The problem is twofold. To

begin with, fungi have not enjoyed the same long-term popularity. For the most part they only appear for a short time each year and in specific locations, and people are traditionally wary of them. So, they are less familiar to us and familiarity is normally the trigger for common naming. There is also a difficulty of distinction. Often a fungus lacks the obvious characteristics or associations which would encourage a common tag.

There is, thankfully, a growing trend to encourage popular names. This will no doubt accelerate as years go by and fungus hunting gains in popularity. Some field guides are better than others at offering common names. There has to be a word of caution though. The object of the 'Binomial System', the method by which every plant is provided with at least two names, a generic family name and a specific name, is to provide a system that is universally accepted and understood. In other words, if you talk to a Russian and an Italian about an Oyster Cap, the odds are that they will look at you blankly. Tell them that the specimen is a *Pleurotus ostreatus*, and recognition will dawn.

Hence there is a use for Latin, the universal scientific language. The system also places different plants in accurate and proper relationship with one another. To judge from their English names, 'Fly Agaric' and 'Blusher' have little in common, but apply their scientific names, *Amanita muscaria* and *A. rubescens*, and the connection becomes clear.

It is therefore worth wrestling with the Latin nomenclature, even if it may seem hard going at first. The names do become familiar quite quickly and can often actually sound logical. *Coprinus disseminatus* implies that one should expect a large number of the specimens spread over an area, whilst *Marasmius alliaceus* smells of onions!

One perennial headache with naming is that official titles tend to change, not quite with the regularity of the seasons, but getting on that way. If you happen to be a member of the British Mycological Society, or some other august body which lays down the names for fungus identification, this is all very serious stuff. To the rest of us, it is a pain in the neck. Here is a simple illustration: the Larch Boletus, an elegant specimen with a slippery, yellowish cap and tubes, and a white ring, used to be called *Boletus elegans*, until someone decided in their wisdom to change it to *Suillus grevillei*. Ask most of the hunters on a foray why this change came about and they haven't a clue, yet we are all stuck with it.

In consequence a book published in the 1960s which is otherwise excellent and reliable will display a number of names that are at odds with those contained in a similar volume published in the 1980s.

The books also tend towards some fairly daunting terms to describe fungi. This is necessary up to a point because very often fine nuances of texture, shape and colour are vital in distinguishing species, and it may be important to know whether a stem is, for instance, warty (verrucose) or mealy (farinose) or powdery (pruinose). If common-or-garden terms were used, one author might talk of a pruinose surface as being powdery, another might call it dusty, and someone else might describe it as frosty. If the accepted terms are used, everyone knows what is what.

It is also true that some of the more worthy tomes use jargon to excess. It is all a question of degree, and it is worth checking on the level of scientific verbiage when you are choosing a field guide. It gets to be very irritating when you have to look up every other word in the glossary before you can understand what is being described.

So, what do you look for in choosing the vital reference book that will be hauled round woods and fields as your mycological bible for years to come? First and foremost it is worth bearing in mind that you *will* have to carry it around, often when you are also weighed down with camera, collecting basket, thermos and sandwiches.

Some of the field books have irritating shortcomings in their handling, which you do not actually find out until it is too late. Beware if a book is large, however excellent its content may be. If it is too big to fit in your pocket, make sure that you can handle it conveniently. Some field guide jackets are provided with a pretty high gloss coating. Ever tried tucking something large and shiny under your arm while you are negotiating fallen logs, low branches, brambles and bogs? After two or three trips, and having dropped the wretched thing so many times you may want to leave it at home, which is defeating the object.

On the other hand, beware of a guide that is too small in format. There is nothing worse than trying to decipher an illustration the size of a postage stamp, particularly in bad light which all too often limits you under trees on a dull autumn day.

The question of how comprehensive the guide is also comes high on the list of important considerations. Personally I would rather carry a thick volume and know that I had a reasonable chance of finding my specimen in it than a thin meagre offering which only provided me with pictures of the commonest types, most of which I probably know anyway.

Above all, before you buy, look hard at the illustrations. Beware of artist's impressions. The only book I know of which has paintings I would trust is the old 1963 Collins *Guide to Mushrooms and Toadstools*, with water colours from the *Flora Agaricina Danica*. These are good, which is more than can be said for some of the other illustrations on the market.

Check also, that the descriptions are thorough and that they are in the same place as the pictures! That may seem silly advice, but it is extremely off-putting to find what looks to be the right picture, only to have to hunt for the explanation that goes with it three or four pages further on.

Finally, have a glance at the fly-leaf and check the author's credentials.

Depending upon how far you want to go with fungus hunting and identifying, there are a number of options for recording what you find. The simplest method is to set out equipped with a camera. Whether you take colour prints or transparencies is a matter of personal choice. The only advice I would give is that print film tends to handle excessive light contrasts more ably than transparency stock, bearing in mind that a lot of the specimens you will find will be in dappled shade.

If you choose to use flash, that problem is largely irrelevant, but remember that subtle colours are treated a lot less sensitively by light from a flash gun, than if you rely on whatever daylight is available.

You will also need to be prepared to go crawling about on the ground, which is generally rather wet and soggy on the knees unless you wear waterproofs or go as I do, equipped with a small plastic sheet to lie on.

The alternative, and perhaps the more aesthetically satisfying solution, is to draw and colour. The best results seem to come from the use of water colours.

Boletus elegans

It is probably worth taking the specimens home to stand as models on a table rather than on a chilly forest floor, not least because you may end up hauling an awful lot of gear around with you to produce *in situ* masterpieces, and dense woodlands are not the most navigable places if you are weighed down with artists' paraphernalia as well as everything else!

It is possible to dry fungi. The vast mycological herbarium at the Royal Botanical Gardens, Kew, is based on dried material. It does not look very pretty, though, and the lush, fat specimens you pick tend to change rather dramatically for the worse. Drying is probably of more value for a scientific record than a personal collection.

It is fun, as well as an important identification exercise, to make spore prints. By laying a fresh cap, gills down, on a piece of clean paper or glass and covering it to prevent draughts from messing up the pattern, you can create an image of the gills. The spores will gently fall out overnight and dust the surface below, which should, incidentally, be of a contrasting colour to the gills. Spraying gently with hair lacquer will preserve the effect.

In whichever way you intend to make your record, there is one golden rule. Always, if possible, identify the specimen where it is growing and write down its name. Do not rely on memory. I have been close to tearing my hair out, having carefully worked out the species of a particular fungus but forgotten to make a note of it. Three weeks later when the photos came back, I had also managed to forget what it was that I first worked out!

2

Past Interest

*Fungi ben mussherons; there be two manners of them, one
maner is deedly and sleeth them that eateth of them and be called
tode stoles, and the other dooth not. They that be noth deedly
have a grosse gleymy moysture that is dysobedyent to nature
and dygestyon, and be peryllous and dredfull to eate and
therefore it is good to eschew them.*

THE GRETE HERBALL OF 1526

They say it was the Greeks who started the fashion of eating mushrooms; or was it the Romans? The short answer is that nobody knows.
They were probably familiar to civilisations that had crumbled to dust
long before the empires of the classical period were even thought of, though
not necessarily for their culinary virtues.

There is strong evidence from comparatively modern tribes of people living
at a primitive level of culture, that certain powers of fungi may have been
recognised from as far back in time as the last Ice Age. Nomadic hunters who
lived in Siberia and whose shamanistic rites were recorded at the turn of the
last century, were well versed in the values of hallucinogenic mushrooms, and
their lifestyle by all accounts may not have been so very different from that of
the Ice Age peoples of south-west Europe. It may well have been this
traditional religious association that triggered the age-old fear of fungi
amongst Celtic and Germanic peoples.

Nonetheless, it was the writers and poets of the classical empires who put
fungi properly on the map.

The first century A.D. produced a dusting of references to fungi, some
quaint, even hilarious, others more sinister. The physician Nicander wrote a
famous passage which begins:

*Let not the evil ferment of the earth which often causes swellings in the
belly or strictures in the throat, distress a man; for when it has grown up
under the viper's hollow track it gives forth poison and hard breathing of
the mouth; men generally call the ferment by the name of fungus, but
different kinds are distinguished by different names; but do thou take the
many-coated head of cabbage, or cut round the twisting stems of rue, or
take the efflorescence which has accumulated on old corroded copper, or
steep the ashes of clematis in vinegar, then bruise the roots of pyrethrum
adding a sprinkling of lye or soda and the leaf of cress which grows in
gardens with the medic plant and pungent mustard, and burn wine-lees or
the dung of the domestic fowl into ashes; then putting your right finger in
your throat to make you sick, vomit forth the baneful pest.*

Bizarre as this prose may seem, it reveals much of the classicists' view. They
were by now well versed in the joys and dangers of eating fungi. Many a
patrician had met an untimely demise after a feast of deadly fungi, prepared in
blissful innocence (or otherwise) by his cook! Yet they had not realised that
the source of the poisoning was the fungus itself. Somehow they imagined
that the plants were innocent of blame, and that the danger came from
unsavoury elements lurking around where they grew. Hence, Nicander's
comments concerning the 'viper's hollow track'.

The Sicilian herbalist and physician, Dioscorides, writing a hundred years
later, followed a similar line:

*Fungi have a twofold difference, for they are either good for food or
poisonous; their poisonous nature depends on various causes, for either
such fungi grow amongst rusty nails or rotten rags, or near serpent's holes,
or on trees producing noxious fruits; such have a thick coating of mucus,
and when laid by after being gathered, quickly become putrid; but others,
not of this kind, impart a sweet taste to sauces. However even these, if
partaken of too freely, are injurious, being indigestible, causing stricture or
cholera. As a safeguard, all should be eaten with a draught of olive oil, or
soda and lye ashes with salt and vinegar, and a decoction of savory or
marjoram, or they should be followed with a draught composed of bird's*

[33]

dung and vinegar, or with a linctus of much honey; for even the edible sorts
are difficult of digestion and generally pass whole with the excrement.

This account is actually less ludicrous than it may seem. Liberal draughts of
olive oil to ensure 'no hold ups on the way through' was quite sensible if not
particularly appetising advice echoed by physicians until much later times.

Great faith was also placed in the efficacy of bird dung. Its neutralising
properties, coupled with those of lye, may well have rendered innocuous the
acids contained in some poisonous fungi. Most households would have kept
domestic chickens, so raw material was on the doorstep. On this small point,
the fourth century physician Galen added a qualifying note. He advocated the
dung of a free-range bird, in preference to that of 'one in confinement'.

The worst fungal toxins fall into a category known as alkaloids, which are
basic in chemical character. The use of vinegar may have made its mark in
containing the effects of these. A comparable substance, tannic acid (as in tea),
is still regarded as a valuable stand-by in the treatment of certain kinds of
alkaloid poisoning.

Why honey? Often fungal poisoning produces burning sensations in the
mouth and throat, for which the honey linctus would have been soothing. So
there was a reason behind the old cures; but with all these dire warnings of the
unpleasant effects of eating fungi, why did the ancients develop an obsession
with them, because obsession it certainly was?

The first and foremost culprit was perhaps sheer boredom at the dining
table. Towards the twilight years of the Roman Empire, all patricians were
expected to 'tighten the belt'. There had been a tradition of excesses
emanating from the kitchens of the city's high society. It was not unusual for
a wealthy citizen to import a few dozen peacocks' brains to serve up as
appetisers for his current 'thrash'. But now money was running short and, in
an effort to combat the excesses of her denizens, Rome's Senate passed
'Sumptuary Laws', which effectively banned any costly or exotic meat dishes
but spared vegetables.

Whether the Romans were encouraged to grow-their-own is not clear, but
the limitations on boars' heads, goose livers, and peacocks' brains may have

driven jaded gourmets to seek new pleasures in the dangerous but delightful sport of fungus cookery.

The cult which accompanied mushroom eating in Imperial Rome was a little excessive. The best-equipped kitchens owned special vessels called *boletaria* for preparing and cooking fungi. The terminology is confusing, because the tags the Romans attached to different kinds of fungi are sometimes used in other contexts today. Their *boleti* were not members of the Boletus family, but all the typical gill-bearing agarics growing on soil. *Suilli* were the pore-bearing specimens, a name which incidentally has now been attached to a modern sub-group of Boletus-type fungi. The Roman gourmet recognised a truffle for what is today, and the title *fungi farnei* was coined for specimens growing on trees.

The *boletarium* was treated with considerable reverence. Woe betide any kitchen servant who employed it for preparing less worthy vegetables. Martial, one of the popular satirists of his day, quipped: 'Although boleti have given me so noble a name, I am now used, I am ashamed to say, for Brussels sprouts.' (Brussels sprouts is, I suspect, a piece of translator's licence.)

The recipes for the preparation of the different kinds of fungi were often quite specific. *Fungi farnei* had to be boiled, then strained dry. They were served with copious amounts of pepper and a delightful condiment, the Worcestershire Sauce of its day. Known as *liquamen*, it was based on fish guts. Salt, curiously, was a rare commodity in ancient Rome, and the liquamen served as a substitute. Tasty stuff no doubt.

Boleti, by contrast, were served raw in a reduced wine-based sauce known as *caroenum*, or stewed in stock with liquamen and pounded pepper. The Romans called them *suilli* apparently because the pigs, given half a league, enjoyed a feast of Boletus.

The Romans demonstrated a distinct weakness for truffles, which were sliced, boiled, transfixed with sticks and part-roasted. This, however, was only the start of the recipe! They were popped into a special saucepan and doused with oil, liquamen, caroenum, seasoning and honey, and boiled once more. As a quick alternative, Roman cookery books also suggested bagging the truffles in pig guts – classical haggis.

Among the most popular *boleti* to be sold in the Roman market, was *Amanita caesarea*. One of those oddities, a wholesome member of the 'Death Cap' brigade, it was truly the mushroom of the Caesars. Caelius Apicus included many references to it in his celebrated cookery manual.

A. caesarea was also innocently responsible for Nero fiddling whilst Rome burned. The story would grace any modern day soap opera. The plot goes roughly thus: the Emperor Claudius, who succeeded the infamous Caligula, showed a strong penchant for women. His fourth, and ill-fated, marriage, was to Agrippina. Each had a child by previous wedlock. Britannicus was Claudius' son by his third wife, and Agrippina brought with her a precocious youth called Nero.

Britannicus was, of course, heir to the laurel leaves, a situation which did not go down well with the ambitious Agrippina. Her easy solution was to murder Claudius by the most crafty means she could devise. Accordingly she employed the services of a notorious lady of the black arts, Locusta. An unholy trio consisting of the empress, Locusta and Claudius' eunuch descended to the imperial kitchens and prepared a dish of *A. caesarea*, which was duly served to Claudius.

The emperor tucked in heartily, unaware that his favourite dish had been laced with the juice of the Death Cap (*A. phalloides*). Claudius was, predictably and almost overnight, elevated to the ranks of the gods and the rest, as they say, is history.

Claudius was by no means the only Roman figure of note to be disposed of through the agency of poisonous fungi, but his demise is probably the best recorded.

The Romans and Greeks also understood the damaging capacity of fungi in agriculture. A red rust fungus, the Red Corn of the Bible, provided a constant plague, and had the early farming lobby knocking regularly on the doors of the Senate. They attributed the problem to various causes: frost, sun and divine retribution. They organised annual processions along the Claudian Way each April 25th to the sacred grove of the god Robigus, where they burnt the entrails of a russet coloured dog in an effort to appease the spirits and ward off the prospects of blight for the coming season. Predictably, the lobbyists kept coming back.

On the other side of the coin, the Classical Age also recognised the therapeutic properties of some fungi. Dioscorides described 'Agaricus' as being efficacious against colds and sores, fractures, liver complaints, asthma, jaundice and hysteria . . . not to mention acrid eructations. 'Agaricus' was not the mushroom we know, but a locally occurring species of *Fomes*, growing on larch trees.

Not surprisingly, it was the enthusiasm of post-Empire Italians that in no small way carried the interest in fungi through to medieval times. It was an Italian director of the Botanical Gardens in Pisa, Caesalpinus, who in 1583 correctly described the toadstool as a fruit. The name 'toadstool', however, is probably of Germanic origin, though the exact derivation is in some doubt. It may be a corruption of the words 'tod stuhl' meaning stalk of death. On the other hand, fungi have long been associated with toads, traditionally thought of as the instruments of witches, and as poisonous creatures. It is a curious fact, though, that English is the only language to distinguish between 'mushrooms' and 'toadstools'. Every other European culture adopts all-embracing terms.

The French botanist Clusius (real name Charles de L'Ecluse) was the first to attempt a serious scientific listing of fungi, but his knowledge was painfully limited, and for a long time the French probably echoed the reticence felt across the English Channel. *The Grete Herball* is in fact of French origin, and it is hardly favourable to fungi. Nonetheless, it was the French who coined the word 'mousseron'. The English court picked up the expression during the fifteenth century, and thus 'mushroom' was derived.

Clusius divided all fungi into two groups, each with an equal number of families – poisonous and edible! He managed to position a number of well-known species correctly.

St George's Mushroom and *Amanita caesarea* went into the edible 'bag', but Jew's Ear, for less than scientific reasons, was maligned as being poisonous. The fungus only grows on elder trees and thus has strong traditional association with Judas Iscariot who allegedly hung himself from an elder tree.

By the time of the English naturalist Gerard, whose immortal *Herbal* was published in 1638, attitudes had changed at least towards Jew's Ear. He recommended it boiled in milk to soothe sore throats. In other respects he was fairly hostile towards fungi:

Few mushrooms are good to be eaten and most of them do suffocate and strangle the eater. Therefore I give my advice unto those that love such strange and new fangled meates to beware of licking honey among thorns lest the sweetness of the one do not countervaile the sharpness and pricking of the other.

If Darwin's daughter felt a mite prudish about the Stinkhorn (*Phallus impudicus*), her diffidence had its precedent! Gerard copied the fungus from a drawing of Clusius, but turned it upside down in his herbal, though with true Elizabethan robustness, he identified it as the Pricke Mushrom (*Fungus Virilis Penis effigie*).

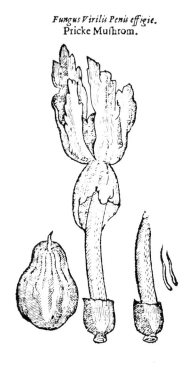

Fungus Virilis Penis effigie.
Pricke Muſhrom.

Phallus impudicus

The attitude of English herbalists like Gerard, Culpeper, who hardly mentions fungi, and Bankes, can have done little to improve public opinion and may be responsible for the suspicious attitude towards fungi that the majority of British people maintain to this day.

Our men of letters hardly bettered the image of the fungus. Tennyson had one of his heroines, Lynette, turn from Gareth as if she had smelled 'a foul-fleshed agaric'. Shelley was no more charitable in *The Sensitive Plant*:

And agarics and fungi, with mildew and mould,
Started like mist from the wet ground cold;
Pale, fleshy, as if the decaying dead
With a spirit of growth had been animated!

Their moss rotted off them, flake by flake,
Till the thick stalk stuck like a murderer's stake
Where rags of loose flesh yet tremble on high,
Inspecting the winds that wander by.

[39]

D. H. Lawrence continued the refrain amongst the later poets:

How beastly the bourgeois is
especially the male of the species –
Nicely groomed, like a mushroom
standing there so sleek and erect and eyeable –
and like a fungus, living on the remains of bygone life,
sucking his life out of the dead leaves of greater life than his
own.

It was left to Elias Fries to put the classification of fungi on a sound scientific footing. Between 1867 and 1884 he compiled the massive *Icones Selectae Hymenomycetae*. His is still the basis of fungal typing today.

Commercial mushroom growing began in the seventeenth century. An anonymous pioneer found that wild mushroom spawn, a portion of the mycelium lifted from a field, could be inoculated into horse manure so that the mushrooms grew in it. As early as 1707 a mycophile named de Tournefort published his method of growing mushrooms on horse manure, a technique that was studiously followed until the twentieth century. One of the persistent limitations of commercial growing was that, until 1894, no one had been able to extract pure mushroom spawn. Two French scientists, Constantin and Matruchot, succeeded but in spite of patents their technique was never applied properly. The honours fell to an American, Duggar, who developed his separate technique in 1905. Mushrooms always used to be grown underground, and although a Swedish mushroom grower suggested, in 1754, that they could be cultivated in greenhouses, the alternative was only fully employed in comparatively recent times.

On the Continent, fungi were truly appreciated by most people, to the extent that certain limitations had to be enforced by law to reduce the number of fatalities brought about by dabbling! In the 1830s, a *Congregazione Speciale di Sanita* was set up in Italy to establish safeguards in the practice of buying and selling fungi. They came up with a fairly draconian seven-point plan, which was placed on the statute books in 1837.

1 In future an *Ispettore di Funghi*, a civil servant versed in mycology, was to attend the market to inspect all mushroom produce.

2 All mushrooms brought into Rome were to be registered under the eye of the *Ispettore*. All the baskets were to be sealed and consigned under escort to a central warehouse for distribution.

3 The fungus market was to be established at a specified place, and anyone found hawking elsewhere in the streets would have their produce confiscated, and be subject to fine or imprisonment.

4 At 7.00 a.m. precisely, all produce was to be laid out on the ground for examination by the *Ispettore*, who would then issue a formal printed permit on payment of one *baiocco* per 10lb of approved produce.

5 Any vendor whose saleable material amounted to less than 10lb would be exempt from the tax levy.

6 Stale fungi from the previous day, along with any 'reject' material not passed as wholesome by the *Ispettore*, were despatched immediately under escort and dumped into the Tiber, as incidentally were any specimens of 'common mushroom'!

7 The *Ispettore* was empowered to fine or imprison anyone who broke the regulations. The same *Ispettore* was required to furnish a detailed weekly report of activities to the Tribunal of Provisions (the equivalent of the Min of Ag).

There is a sombre if tragically funny postscript. A comparable system was established in Paris where, shortly after the scheme opened, a newspaper cutting identified the death of *L'Inspecteur du Fungi*. Cause of death ... mushroom poisoning. The Mushroom Inspector has, however, become an established figure on the Continent. In Switzerland, there are currently about 500 inspectors checking commercially marketed fungi during the season.

In England, though, there is no parallel. Victorian mushroom enthusiasts like the Reverend Worthington Smith made valiant efforts to educate us into the delights of mushroom eating. Books were written extolling the virtues of the edible fungi, including C. D. Badham's *Esculent Funguses of England*, published in 1863. All was in vain though. As a nation we remain stubborn and illogical mycophobes.

3
Mushroom Biology

Think of a piece of cotton wool, teased and stretched until all the fibres are separated into a loose skein but with constant parting and rejoining, rather like a map of the London Underground, and you have a picture of the working heart of a fungus. The analogy with the Underground is not entirely inappropriate, because the threads of the skein are hollow tubes forming a highly efficient transport and communication network.

The whole system is the *mycelium* and the individual threads are *hyphae*. Because it does not function in the same way as the tissues of a green plant – it has no need of light to carry out its daily routines – the mycelium is much less obtrusive than the vegetative part of a cabbage plant or a chestnut tree. There are, incidentally, some green fungi but their colour is produced by chemicals other than the chlorophyll of a true green plant. The fungus has no need of light-gathering organs like leaves, so it has no use for a leafy stem, one of the purposes of which is to raise the leaves to a position where they can receive goodly amounts of light on their surfaces. Only occasionally does the mycelium produce something equivalent to a stalk, and that is solely to raise the fruiting body into the air.

In consequence, the cotton-wool-like mass is usually only to be found by probing in the leaf litter, or prising up rotten bark. Unlike genuine cotton wool, the threads are of markedly differing thicknesses, and what tend to be obvious are the larger 'trunk' strands.

The finer hyphae, each slimmer than a strand of cobweb silk, merge almost imperceptibly into the 'host'. Generally the mycelium is white, though in some fungi it is distinctly coloured. It produces very obvious brown 'boot-laces' in the Honey Fungus (*Armillaria mellea*).

The expression 'host' is a carefully chosen one, because fungi are not free living. Unlike a green plant, which needs the soil only as an anchoring point, and as a reservoir of water and of minute quantities of valuable minerals, the fungus is dependent wholly on some other organism for its survival.

The host need not be alive. Only a limited number of fungi are true parasites, drawing from a living animal or plant. The great majority are technically known as *saprophytes*. Put in another way, it means that they are rubbish disposers. Without fungi and bacteria, the world's surface would very rapidly become immersed in plant and animal remains. Think of all the leaves which woodland trees deposit in autumn, yet by the following summer they have somehow 'evaporated'. A tree trunk may lie on the forest floor for a year or two, but slowly it is disintegrating. Its tissues are becoming softer and collapsing into ever smaller fragments. Much of this is down to the activity of fungal mycelia, which very quickly invade the dead tree.

The speed with which fungi become established, given the right conditions, is apparent if you happen to leave a loaf of bread (one without preservatives) in a polythene bag in warm damp conditions. Within a couple of days, blue penicillin and black dotted pin-mould will be making themselves obvious. Warm humid conditions and lack of draughts are the keys to happy living for fungi!

Clearly, the life style of the fungi is a remarkably efficient one. They are some of the oldest plants on earth, and in spite of the apparent simplicity of form in their mycelial construction they are extremely successful. They have colonised practically every corner of the globe. They live in the sea and in fresh water. Their spores are resilient, surviving very low temperatures, heat and drought. The air we breathe contains countless millions of fungal spores. They will happily invade our homes, attacking anything from the floorboards to the skin between our toes. Fungi will even live in intimate and amicable relationship with other plants, in a style that is mutually beneficial and which allows them to colonise such unlikely habitats as bare rock faces.

What, then, is the secret of success? The key lies in the way in which the fungus goes about its business, and this is not apparent until it is under the microscope.

In its most simple state, the fungus consists of a single living cell. Yeasts fall into this category. A pin-head drop of bakers' yeast is actually made up of millions of separate cells which, under the right conditions, spend all their working lives feeding, dividing and producing carbon dioxide. It is this gas which is responsible for making the dough rise.

Most of the Higher Fungi, though, are multicellular, forming their complex networks of hyphal threads. These are in effect enormous cells containing many nuclei, which have formed into living tunnels. In a parasitic fungus, the threads either penetrate or run between the cells of the host plant. The damage to the host is caused by chemicals exuded at the tips of the hyphae, the active working points of the threads. The chemicals are enzymes, the purpose of which is to dissolve the tissues around them. The hyphae are restricted in the form of material they can make use of, so solids cannot be absorbed, only solubles. Once the cell walls of the host off which the fungus is living, are broken down into a convenient 'juice', all is drawn in through the hypha and put to use in forming new fungal tissue and the sugars which the fungus uses as a source of energy.

Frequently the effect of parasitic fungal attack is to kill the host. It is an insidious process, but an extremely effective one, and it can cause the eventual downfall of huge trees as well as untold damage to crops. It is responsible for diseases in human beings, like ringworm, athlete's foot and thrush. On the other side of the coin, parasitic fungi like penicillin can be put to good use because they attack selectively. Among the hosts for which they have a strong liking are the bacteria which cause infection.

Saprophytic fungi operate in a similar manner, but they are designed to go to work on dead material and organic rubbish.

Regardless of life style, the fungal mycelium will grow and invade more and more of its surroundings until the living gets tough. Under certain adverse conditions such as drought or frost, the fungus will simply close down business and go into a resting period. However, if the source of sustenance is used up and if the fungus's system is alerted in other ways, such as by the climatic change in autumn, the fungus will be triggered to assume it needs to reproduce itself. This will, in effect, enable it to move to a fresh location with new host material to build on once more. To effect this replication it needs to produce, in Higher Fungi, mushrooms and toadstools. The process is a little more complicated, though, than merely generating a fruiting body from the existing mycelium. It involves a little sexual foreplay!

A single microscopic spore liberated from a mushroom can germinate to produce a mycelium. That structure cannot, however, go on to produce another generation of spores by itself without some rearrangement of the nuclei inside.

In some fungi, like bread mould (*Mucor*) and many of the Ascomycetes, the spores bear one of two possible combinations of genes. There is no realistic parallel to be drawn with the eggs which become males and females in the animal world, but the analogy is helpful to understanding what happens. The spores germinate into either (+) or (−) strains of mycelium, which to all intents and purposes look identical. Before a mycelium can produce a sporophore, a fruiting body, a (+) strain must combine with (−). In the Basidiomycetes, separate (+) and (−) strains are infrequent but, within a mycelium, nuclei have to fuse in pairs and then divide up before spores are ready for liberation.

Ascomycetes and Basidiomycetes differ in the way the spores are produced. In Ascomycetes, the microscopic 'nursery area' is a flask-shaped container, the ascus, from which eight ripe spores are eventually ejected. In Basidio-mycetes, the nursery is a little knob called the basidium, on which typically four spores grow like teats on a cow's udder. It is worth stressing that we are not discussing anything which you can see with the naked eye. All is happening on an extremely small scale, either in or on the fruiting body.

In a typical mushroom like *Agaricus*, the sequence of events goes some-thing like this: a number of hyphae become very densely enmeshed at one point on the mycelium, so that they form a small whitish 'bump' under the soil surface. This first stage of the fruiting body grows at a faster rate on top than underneath, and thus the cap, or *pileus*, becomes distinct from the stalk, or *stipe*, forming a little round 'bun'.

The stalk begins to expand lengthways, and within the cap area a space forms. At this juncture, the fruiting body has emerged through the soil surface and is the object commonly referred to as a 'button mushroom'. Inside the roof of the space, the gills are begining to grow, and it is from the surface of these thin vertical plates that the spores will be launched on their fragile journey.

Until this stage, the cap and the gills are protected from the ravages of the outside world by a sheath of tissue, known as the veil or *velum*. This veil goes over the top of the cap and also forms the base of the gill cavity. Now, the cap begins to expand into the umbrella-shape of the mature mushroom, and as it does so the veil becomes ever more stretched until it tears apart, freeing the gills for the first time to the outside air. The veil fragment attached to the stem is the familiar 'ring'.

In many families, the cap expands in such a way that no veil remnants are left, and in the Cortinarius group the tissue stretches into a cobwebby gauze, traces of which remain on the stem after rupture. At the other extreme, in the Amanita group, the veil is double skinned. The inner layer, known as the partial veil, attaches to the stem and forms a characteristic ring, but the outer layer, the total veil, attaches lower down at the top of the bulbous base. When the cap expands this tears and leaves a loose bag called the *volva*.

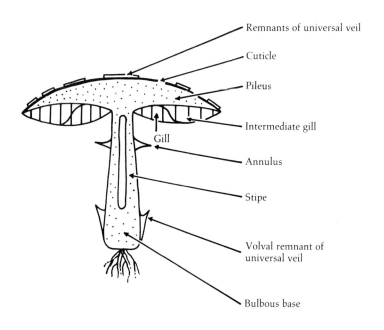

Remnants of universal veil

Cuticle

Pileus

Intermediate gill

Gill

Annulus

Stipe

Volval remnant of universal veil

Bulbous base

SECTION THROUGH GENERALISED AGARIC

The gill surface is effectively the core of the mushroom. A fertile layer, the *hymenium*, grows over and covers it. Thousands upon thousands of minute hyphal tips form club-shaped *basidia*, which function like rocket-launching gantries. Each basidium sends out typically four, but occasionally two, even more minuscule 'pegs' from its tip, and each peg bears a spore. When the spores ripen they are launched horizontally to a very precise distance, so that they lose momentum exactly midway between one gill and its neighbour.

Gravity takes over and the spore goes into free fall, until the air currents catch it and it drifts away to start the cycle all over again. If it chances to settle in some suitable spot it germinates, sprouting a little hypha which slowly grows into a new mycelium.

There are, within the Basidiomycete group, variations on the theme. In the Bracket Fungi, the hymenium is most commonly found on the under surface, and is enclosed in tubes. In the simplest forms, like *Coriolus*, which develop as flat crusts, the fertile layer is on the upper surface. In *Hydnum* and its relatives, the hymenium covers the spines under the cap. Puff Balls develop with the hymenium totally enclosed in a flask-shaped fruiting body, the *peridium*, whose function is to protect a fertile mass of spores and hyphal threads, the *gleba*. The peridium either degenerates all over, as it does in the Giant Puff Ball, or it opens by a distinct pore at the top. In the Stinkhorns, the spore-bearing layer is carried up into the air from a partially submerged gelatinous 'egg', and the spores are removed by flies from a decidedly whiffy slime. It may smell repulsive to the likes of you and me, but if you happen to be born a bluebottle the aroma is impossible to resist.

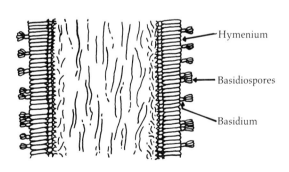

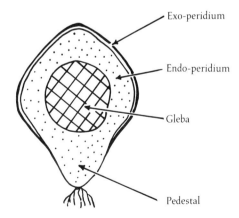

SECTION THROUGH MUSHROOM GILL

SECTION THROUGH GENERALISED 'PUFF BALL' GASTEROMYCETE

Hymenium

Basidiospores

Basidium

Exo-peridium

Endo-peridium

Gleba

Pedestal

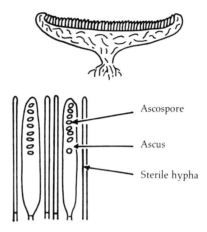

SECTION THROUGH FRUITING BODY OF PEZIZA
AND MAGNIFIED SECTION OF FERTILE LAYER

In the last group of Basidiomycetes, the small rather odd collection of Jelly Fungi (Tremellales), the hymenium develops on a gelatinous fruiting body and, under the microscope, the basidia are more complicated, being divided vertically or horizontally by fragile walls called *septa*.

The Cup Fungi (Peziza) are the simplest of the Ascomycetes. Their spores are formed, not on the surface of a projection, but inside a flask-shaped *ascus*. The fertile hymenium bearing these asci is spread over the upper surface of the cup. Inside each ascus flask eight ascospores develop, bathed in a fluid which is retained under pressure. When the spores are ripe, the neck of the ascus is designed to disintegrate with shock stimulus. This is usually triggered by a rain drop falling on the cup surface. The spores are squirted out into the damp air currents.

There is, of course, quite a lot of structural variation within the Ascomycetes. In the tuberous forms, including truffles, the hymenium is folded inside the fertile part of the tuber, whilst in the Morels and Helvellas it is folded into the shape of the cap, which may be anything from saddle-like to vaguely phallic.

Spores are very important features if you are getting down to heavy identification. You do, of course, need a microscope for this kind of exercise, and it is really only for the dedicated few. Spore colour is often apparent by looking at the gills or pores, but for a really accurate assessment a spore print is vital.

It is in the Agaric fungi that spore identification is most often of use. Cut off the stem and place the cap, gills downwards, on a piece of clean white paper. Cover it with a mixing bowl, or some other protection to keep the air currents at bay.

The set-up needs to be left overnight but by morning the spores will have been shed, and will have made a clear bicycle-wheel pattern on the paper.

Assuming that you possess a microscope and the appropriate bits and pieces of equipment to go with it, scrape some of the spores from the paper with the edge of a clean square coverslip, and press them down on a slide. Providing that you have them in a fairly thick mass, the spore shade can be checked against a suitable chart.

One further useful test of coloration is achieved with a mixture known as Melzer's Iodine (recipe on p. 154). One group of spores produces what is called an amyloid reaction and turn blue-black, others are dextrinoid and turn russety-brown. A good field guide will sometimes refer to spores as having one or other of these reactions.

By examining a thinned number of spores in a drop of suitable mounting fluid, like lactophenol, or a 10% solution of glycerine, important features can be established which, once again, the more detailed field guides will describe. The spore may be identified by its shape, or the possession of warts, spines, ridges and other features on its microscopic surface.

These refinements are for the truly dedicated mycophile. For most people out to distinguish their Lactarius from their Russula, frankly they are unnecessary bits of scientific know-how.

In many fungi, the mycelium seems to grow in a fairly haphazard fashion, wending its way through leaf litter or under bark without any particular pattern to its growth. In such cases, the fruiting bodies pop up more or less at random. In a number of species, however, including common types like Fairy

Ring Champignon (*Marasmius oreades*) and Spotted Tough Shank (*Collybia maculata*), the process is more regular and eventually forms the characteristic 'fairy rings'.

In its first establishing season, the mycelium produces sporophores in a dense cluster. During the following year, it spreads in a radial pattern, leaving the older part of the mycelium to die off towards the centre. The sporophores arise at the extremities, where the new growth is active, and hence a ring appears. The ring expands with every season, and in some instances, including *M. oreades*, the activity of the mycelium seems to stimulate the grass in its vicinity to grow more lush. Thus the signs of the ring become apparent in summer before the mushrooms emerge. These rings can grow to a great age. There is a famous one in eastern France which has spread to a diameter of more than 300 metres, and is said to be about 700 years old.

With all the millions of spores floating around in the air, it would be natural to ask why the world does not clog up, knee deep in fungi. A record of an air sample taken near Cardiff some years ago included 123,000 fungal spores per cubic yard (about 0.75 cubic metres). Luckily most of them have very precise needs in their germination and feeding.

Many fungi are known to develop a close inter-relationship with the roots of flowering plants. This is not a host-parasite dependence, but a mutually beneficial symbiotic arrangement, called a *mycorrhiza*. Such is the advantage to the host plant, that modern techniques of planting and growing forest trees demand the inoculation of the seedling with a mycorrhizal fungus. The skill lies in selecting the fungus to which it is best suited, before planting out. Exactly how, if at all, the fungus benefits, and the extent of mycorrhizal associations in a forest is uncertain. The presence or absence of the special roots on a host plant, which determine if the mushroom you have found growing in tantalising proximity to a birch or an oak is actually mycorrhizal, is largely in the realms of guesswork. If someone informs you, knowingly, that a particular specimen is mycorrhizal, take it with a pinch of salt. The advice may be wishful thinking.

Since the last century, the 'Mecca' of the amateur mycologist has been the headquarters of the British Mycological Society. It is currently lodged in part of a rather pretty collection of Victorian buildings by the Thames at Kew. This is also the official home of the International Mycological Institute where they take fungi very seriously indeed. By and large, the fungi they attend to are not the large Basidiomycetes which you and I are interested in, but the tens of thousands of micro-fungi which make up the bulk of this enormous category of plants.

Kew is a gene bank, as well as a place of research. Fungi from all over the world are stored in perpetuity, in suspended animation. The mycelium and spores of a specimen frozen to the giddy depths of $-190°C$ in liquid nitrogen are reluctant to take much interest in life, yet they survive technically for decades without change. One of the objects of research is to establish the best ways of freezing material, retaining not only its viability and morphological appearance, but also its chemical and physiological properties, which are often changed under such severe treatment. Why go to all the trouble? There are something in the order of a quarter of a million species of fungi *known* worldwide, with some 13,000 stored by the Institute. Some day, in a changed world, we may need to resurrect some of them, perhaps in order to catalyse some future growth strain or to help alleviate a plague.

Today, the precise effects of strains of fungi often have to be analysed for commercial reasons. Did you know that micro-fungi can get into the fuel tanks of aircraft and clog up the engines? Mercifully, until researching the television series, I didn't. I am relieved also to report that the Institute and their research teams are on hand to stop your holiday jet falling out of the sky with an attack of the nasties. Less dramatically, the Institute will resolve technical problems on anything from the blue in Stilton cheese to developments in penicillin technology.

In the nitrogen storage room, vast stainless steel tanks looking like old-fashioned wash boilers breathe white smoke which falls eerily to the ground.

To remove the lids and delve inside requires the donning of heavy gloves. At the temperatures involved, contact between the metal and bare skin will strip the latter in seconds. Inside, the rows of vials containing their cryogenic cargo patiently await resurrection.

To guard against the risk of break-down in the liquid nitrogen units, the Institute store their collection in two other ways. Each specimen effectively has fail-safe back-up.

Specimens are freeze dried and stored at normal temperature in sealed ampoules. Under more old-fashioned preservation methods, cultures are also grown on agar slopes and then covered with mineral oil. This allows the specimen to breathe, but deters unwanted visitors like bacteria and mites.

The International Mycological Institute is the largest centre concerned with the systematic study and recording of fungi in the world. In their more conventional records room are avenues of mobile shelving, filled with paper bags containing pressed material and reeking gently of mothballs. In the high-tech version along the corridor, the same information is housed on the tapes of a vast computerised data-base. Locked in its electronic circuits are the secrets of location, nomenclature, poisonous properties, culture methods and so on.

Close by, at the Royal Botanic Gardens, there is a vast herbarium where fruiting bodies of all the larger fungi are dried and stored. The place looks like a library. Instead of books, there are lockers filled with everything from the biggest brackets to the tiniest agarics. If you find a specimen that really proves impossible to identify, Kew will sort out the problem, although they stress gently that their real work is not in resolving the dilemmas of amateur enthusiasts. They receive about 6,000 specimens a year to identify, which is quite enough to keep them happy.

The talk which lights up eyes at Kew is of such esoteric business as bio-technology, bio-deterioration and plant pathology. Aflatoxins is a useful buzzword to bandy about – something to do with fungi that attack nuts and can cause a nasty case of gippy-tummy. Yet it is vital stuff. Electrical components, concrete, plastics, all suffer from the attacks of fungi. If your TV set fails to work, the culprit may well be a mildew of minute dimensions that has set up home between the contacts somewhere deep in its bowels, feeding happily off equally minute amounts of moisture and dust particles. The mycologists at Kew will sort the problem out.

Sometimes the members of the present-day British Mycological Society could be accused of forgetting that it was founded in Victorian times by enthusiastic amateur fungus collectors. The centenary of the society is beckoning, in 1996. Nowadays, they aim to strike a reasonable balance between the needs of the amateur who wants to enjoy himself for a day in the woods, and the desire of the professional to project a modern high-tech organisation involved in a subject that provides huge value to industry and agriculture.

Unfortunately, some of the leaders of fungal forays seem to have their feet more firmly planted in the latter camp than the former. However, if you find it difficult to locate a local group going in search of fruiting bodies, then the British Mycological Society (address on page 158) will point you in the right direction.

When all is said and done, knowing the technicalities of how a fungus goes about its business is far from vital to having a good time identifying mushrooms and toadstools. It may, however, serve to make these unique and truly fascinating life-forms a little more familiar when you next go out with your basket and book of words.

4
Mushrooms for Eating

Collecting and preparing wild mushrooms has to be one of the most delightful excursions in the realms of cookery. Fungi can offer as many textures, colours and bouquets to enhance your cuisine, as you could wish for. Never be misled into imagining that all fungi taste the same. The flavours they have to offer range from the most delicate hint of mushroom in the Ink Caps, through the piquancy of some Boletus species, to the unique, heady aroma and taste of the truffles.

In the British Isles, we are blessed with a generous variety of edible fungi, yet their potential is undervalued, even scorned. It would be unwise to suggest that the beginner experiments with the length and breadth of the range, ironically because we are spoilt for choice. It is essential, as with any wild food, to know what you are eating. Hence, I am going to offer a Top Twenty that are entirely safe, mouthwateringly delicious, and easy to spot.

As a nation, we tend to base our immediate assessment of a strange fungus, on whether its look, smell and feel bear any resemblance to a 'shop mushroom'. It is in fact a rather unfortunate 'yardstick', because more people have come to grief by confusing dangerous species with *Agaricus campestris* (the country cousin of the shop-bought cultivated species), than with almost any other. Collecting truly 'toadstool-like' specimens from the woods, and cooking them, has a minor track record of misfortune, that pales by comparison. Recently, I trudged home with some specimens of Wood Blewit (*Lepiota nuda*) and showed them to a lady who is otherwise quite catholic in her eating habits. Yet her response to my beautiful meal, courtesy of the copse down the road, was: 'Ugh, you can't eat those. They're *blue*!'

We miss out! Many continental countries leave us in the shade when it

Boletus badius

comes to understanding the delights of wild mushrooms. France and Italy abound with delicious traditional recipes, for a variety of fungi.

Most of the types listed in this chapter were located and broadcast in the course of making the Channel Four television series. I have collected, cooked and eaten all of them. I have enjoyed the experience enormously, and never once has my stomach hinted at indignation.

This record has to be down to following the rules with some degree of sanity. The number of times I come across otherwise intelligent people collecting unfamiliar specimens for the table, on the lame excuse that they 'look all right', never ceases to amaze me. There are many weird and wonderful old wives' tales about fungi. Forget them! There is only one yardstick for eating fungi, and that is to gain sound experience in the proper identification of what you are about to pop into your mouth.

The oldest fallacy is that edible fungi peel, whilst poisonous varieties do not. It is true that the common mushroom peels easily, but so regrettably does the Death Cap (*A. phalloides*), as a number of victims have discovered to their cost.

Many people still quote the old misconception that poisonous fungi blacken a silver spoon. This probably stems from the alchemistic principle that silver, a precious metal, will draw evil substances from an object and absorb them. The common mushroom produces no reaction with silver, but neither, once again, does Death Cap.

Brightly coloured fungi are generally viewed as being unwholesome, particularly if they are coloured red, the sign of danger. In the main, that happens to be true, though there are probably more reddish-hued Russula species worthy of the table than otherwise. However, the majority of the really nastily dangerous fungi are notable for their inconspicuous colouring.

The cut flesh changing colour is also supposed to be indicative of a suspect nature, probably stemming from the old adage that poisons react to the light. As with so many of these quaint notions, there is an element of truth. The pores of the inedible *Boletus calopus* react in this way, and the dangerously poisonous *B. purpureus* turns an alluring shade of blue when bruised. However, the superbly palatable *B. badius* also has pores which turn blue, as do those of a number of other edible members of the family. Recently I was out with someone who claimed to be an 'old hand' at collecting wild mushrooms, but who was quite insistent, in contradiction with the homespun theory, that any Boletus which bruised green was OK to eat. All of which goes to prove that changing colour means not a thing. Sometimes it supports the adage, sometimes not.

Another claim which can rapidly lead to catastrophe is that if the specimen has been nibbled by animals, it is all right for humans to eat. Many animals, particularly herbivores, seem to have a built-in immunity to certain poisons which affect human beings. Rabbits, not to mention slugs and other creepy-crawlies, will often make a meal of Death Cap and live to see another day. We humans very definitely would not.

The only certain tale, is the one which most country people of bygone days followed by instinct: learn what is good and what is not from someone who already knows with first hand experience. Even then, until you are absolutely sure, double check with a good field guide. Follow this golden rule, and you are unlikely to go wrong.

To put the edible and poisonous fungi into some kind of perspective, very few of the 3500 larger species to be found in Britain are poisonous in any way. At the other end of the gastronomic spectrum, a rather more extensive block are edible and good. The overwhelming bulk, though, are neither one thing nor the other. They are harmless if eaten, but are unsuitable for the kitchen because they are unpalatable. They lack the taste or the texture to make them attractive. They may shrivel away to nothing the moment they hit the pan, or they may remain tough and woody in spite of all the tricks of cooking you throw at them. They may be slimy or bitter, acid or peppery. To smell pleasantly of curry or coconut is one thing, but how many people will relish the odour of mouse droppings wafting off the plate?

Nonetheless, should the wild mushroom gourmet accidently include a 'rogue' specimen of this kind with his dinner, he will neither vomit, nor turn blue, nor go into convulsions. There will probably be no after effects, and at worst he might have noticed an unpleasant taste or aroma.

Carleton Rea and R. H. Wakefield – Victorian enthusiasts on an expedition

So, what is needed in the way of equipment, if we are going to pick for the table? Not a lot. The ideal container is a Sussex trug, or a flat, open-weave basket. Mushrooms bruise very easily, particularly the more delicate ones, and it is best not to pile them one on top of another. Once a fungus (in common with most vegetables) is bruised, it will spoil much faster than if it has been handled with care and allowed to reach the kitchen table undamaged.

Polythene bags should be given a wide berth, and so should plastic carriers and even plastic picnic boxes if they are unventilated. Air needs to circulate round the specimens, otherwise condensation builds up and they can rapidly become mushy and stale. That is particularly true if the air is warm and damp (in a heated car on the way home). The flat basket may not carry as many specimens as a deeper container, but it is better to trudge back to the car several times with a single layer in your basket, and spread them out in the boot, rather than trying to cram layer upon layer.

Some enthusiasts, with an eye to conservation, will tell you that it is better to cut the mushroom off by its stalk, rather than pulling it up, because uprooting it allegedly damages the vegetative mycelium under the ground. Take no notice. The all-important mycelium is largely undamaged by pulling up the stem, but what is more important, you might leave behind an important identification feature. Sometimes, though, it is not possible to remove the mushroom without assistance, particularly if it is growing out of the side of a tree, in which case a sharp knife with a proper sheath is indispensable. Cut the stem cleanly as near to the base as possible.

Incidentally, since it is well-nigh impossible to extricate soil and grit from between the gills, once they have wriggled in there, it is a very good idea to brush off any surplus soil from the base of the stem before up-ending the specimen. Few things are more likely to put you off the prizes you have carried home in triumph than a mouthful of grit.

Once the crop is collected, it is advisable to get it home as soon as possible. The temptation, of course, is to collect everything in sight, as soon as you set foot in the woods and fields, but it is best, if you intend to spend the day foraging, to wait until nearer going-home time, than to tote a basketful around for hours. The contents may end up looking a little on the tired side.

Langermannia gigantea – the famous Giant Puff Ball

Which brings me to my Top Twenty. Let me just repeat that this book is not a field guide, and my descriptions will not necessarily provide all the relevant details. Unless you are genuinely confident that you know them already, do check them carefully in a book which is designed specifically for that purpose, the pros and cons of which we discussed in Chapter 1.

In late summer, before the real autumn season has got under way, the first variety to look out for is the Giant Puff Ball (*Langermannia gigantea*). It is a real eye-goggler of a specimen, and is a 'must' if you are going to class yourself as a proper wild mushroom eater. From an innocent-looking puff ball no more than a couple of centimetres across, the fully matured fruiting body can grow to a massive 60 cm or more, a huge whitish, leathery creation attached to the soil by a straggly little umbilical thread, which surprisingly is all that connects the ball with its source of food. Giant Puff Balls can weigh over a kilo, with enough flesh on them to feed a football team.

Langermannia is only suitable for eating when it is firm and pure white all through. Once the gleba, the spore mass, starts to ripen and becomes discoloured inside, it is past its best. According to somebody's calculations, a large specimen will then proceed to puff out seven billion spores, give or take the odd one or two. The whole exodus takes a week or more, once the outer wall has started to break away. The process is made more efficient because the attaching cord breaks and the ball is free to roll around. Giant Puff Balls usually grow on the edges of woods, or in grassy places, on the soil. We found ours in the densest part of a nettle bed, which is probably why they lived to a ripe old age, and why I spent the rest of the day itching!

In Victorian and Edwardian times Giant Puff Ball used to find its way on to the menu at the Freemasons' Tavern in West London. It was always served up there on state occasions. The traditional way of cooking is to cut the ball into slices, like a loaf, dip it into beaten egg, and then coat it with breadcrumbs, season and sauté quickly in a little butter.

Another more adventurous suggestion is to hollow out the whole puffball, chop the centre part finely and mix with chestnut stuffing. Return the mixture to the shell and drape with back bacon rashers. Wrap the ball in foil and bake in the oven at 170°C. The texture is quite unlike that of a common mushroom, almost reminiscent of sweetbreads. Utterly delicious!

Once the season really gets under way, the choice of woods and fields is yours, but since there is so much confusion about the Field Mushroom, the open pasture may be a good place to begin.

However, if you still have romantic notions of nipping off one sweet autumn morning and collecting a basketful of Field Mushrooms from the nearest paddock, you may be sadly disappointed. With the effects of spraying pasture with chemicals having taken its toll, the 'common mushroom' is these days a distinct rarity. It is amazing how many farmers will tell you, 'Field behind my orchard had loads of 'em . . . last year!'

If you actually manage to find it before anybody else does, *Agaricus campestris* (the Field Mushroom) is really quite distinctive. The first point to remember is that it is a fleshy mushroom. If you come across delicate little white jobs in the field, then they are not what you are looking for! The cap measures about seven to ten centimetres across when mature, and is white or possibly creamy. It is either scaly or smooth, but is definitely meaty.

The most significant features to look for are underneath. Dig up the specimen complete – you can usually poke it out with your finger – and look at the gills. Even in a very young specimen, they should be a deep pink, later becoming dark brown. Don't be surprised if there is no ring on the stem. Even if the book describes one, it is a rather half-hearted thing, which soon disappears.

There are a number of other Agaricus species which grow in pasture, including the Horse Mushroom (*A. arvensis*), and *A. macrosporus*. Both possess fine distinctions which it is worth getting to know, but a casual collector would probably lump both as 'horse mushrooms' or large field mushrooms.

Both make excellent dishes, and tend to be more strongly flavoured than the Field Mushroom. Don't be put off by the slight smell of ammonia in *A. macrosporus*. It goes away on cooking.

It is also worth looking out for some of the tastier woodland species of Agaricus, including the Prince (*A. augustus*), which smells strongly of almonds, and the Wood Mushroom (*A. silvicola*), which smells equally of aniseed.

If there is a message of warning about the Agaricus family, it is to check carefully any which stain yellow on cutting, until you are quite sure of their identity. Unfortunately several good varieties, including the Wood Mushroom, react in this way, but so also do some nasty members; whereas any that do not turn yellow, are safe. Incidentally, although this is not a chapter on poisonous fungi, it is worth pointing out that 'nasty' in this case means at worst a bad tummy upset.

Before plunging into the woods to find new delights, there are a couple more easy-to-spot specimens which you are likely to find in the open. Look out for one of them as you drive around the autumn lanes. The Shaggy Ink Cap (*Coprinus comatus*) is one of those eye-catching specimens which I defy anyone to confuse. It is also known as the Judge's Wig, because in its young state it has a strong similarity to the courtroom apparel. For some reason, it

Coprinus comatus

Top] *Agaricus augustus*

Bottom] *Agaricus silvicola*

seems to favour mown roadside verges, though it does rear up in the middle of pastures, and on lawns. A very pretty toadstool, it needs to be eaten when young. Any trace of black on the cap means that it is past its best. It should either be pure white, or have a delicate shade of pink on the gills, at most.

It was the first toadstool I ever tasted, and if for no other reason, it holds a particular place in my affections. The main criticism of it is its lack of strong flavour. It is in fact very mild, which also perhaps makes it a good one for newcomers to 'cut their teeth on'. Cooked in the right way, though, it makes a delightful and delicate appetiser. All parts can be used. Cut off the base of the stem, and then quarter the whole thing lengthwise. There is no need to scrape away the scales, but the apex of the cap may need a little attention where it has pushed through the soil.

The texture is very tender, and needs only the briefest of cooking. The best recipe I know is to sauté the caps for a few seconds in butter with some softened, chopped shallot, then add a cupful of white wine, a pinch of nutmeg and a little seasoning. Serve with croûtons.

Staying out in the open, the Fairy Ring Champignon (*Marasmius oreades*) should be familiar to most people. It is a little, flattish-topped mushroom, often with a broad hump or umbo, tan-coloured when wet, but drying a paler buff. The gills are creamy-coloured and widely spaced, alternating with shorter intermediates, and the mushroom is said to smell of fresh sawdust, occasionally with almondy overtones. Its stem also tends to penetrate below ground for some distance like a little root.

The only possible confusion is with a pair of specimens, *Clitocybe rivulosa* and *C. dealbeata*, of similar size, and which in company with *M. oreades* tend to grow in troops or rings, in short pasture and lawns. The colour of these is much paler, though, more an off-white, the gills are crowded and decurrent, and there is no 'rooting' of the stem. Both are dangerously poisonous, so are worth keeping in mind, but the distinctions are sufficient to make separating Fairy Ring Champignon fairly easy.

It is an excellent flavouring fungus, with the added advantage that it dries and stores well. In days gone by, when any self-respecting country wife knew of its worth, she would remove the stalks, which tend to be tough, string the caps together with a thread of cotton and a darning needle, and hang them across the rafters of her kitchen to dry. They can be ground up, or bottled whole, in an air tight container. Some London delicatessens are now stocking *Marasmius* again, just as they did before the last war, though it has never gone out of fashion across the Channel.

Traditional steak and kidney pie recipes very often included Fairy Ring Champignon. One of the more vociferous of Victorian fungus hunters, the Reverend Worthington G. Smith, was also full of praise for the mushroom in its own right, advocating a straightforward broiling in butter. This method, he insisted, is 'guaranteed to produce a flavour exquisitely rich and delicious . . . which must be tasted to be understood.'

Worthington Smith was nothing if not besotted with wild mushrooms. He was one of those foolhardy eccentrics who led a charmed life, because he seems to have eaten practically everything his eye set upon, and although he suffered accountably in the process, he lived to a ripe old age! He made one of his not infrequent blunders with *Marasmius oreades*.

According to his memoirs, he collected a specimen which with hindsight he identified as *M. urens*, the 'False Champignon'. He gathered the mushrooms for his supper, but found them unusually hot. Blame was at first attributed to the addition of too much pepper by his long-suffering elderly cook. However, as the night wore on, Reverend Smith suffered burning sensations in the throat and stomach, accompanied by headache and dizziness, and was violently ill. It did not staunch his passion!

Last of my late summer and early autumn grassland favourites are the Parasol Mushrooms (*Lepiota procera*) and the rather more common Shaggy Parasols (*L. rhacodes*). Again, difficult to confuse with anything else, the tall, elegant *L. procera* grows in gardens, on the edges of forests, on firebreaks, and in grassy places near trees. *L. rhacodes* (of which there is also a garden variety) is more familiar in open woodlands and shrubby areas.

All three have tough, woody stems with rings and bulbous bases, and large scaly caps, quite distinct from those of the Amanitas with their patches. The gills are whitish coloured and free from the stem. If you look closely, a little clear trough runs around its apex.

Top] *Lepiota rhacodes*

Marasmius oreades Bottom] *Boletus edulis*

If you are going to eat Parasols, get rid of the stem, which is too tough to be palatable. The younger caps are dome-shaped, and are just waiting for a savoury filling. A whole tomato makes a colourful effect, or a little stuffing – really whatever takes your fancy. Wrap each cap in foil with a generous dab of butter on top, and pop in the oven at about 160°C for 20 minutes. Once your dinner guests have recovered from the culture shock, they will immediately be converted to the delights of wild mushroom cookery.

For a lunchtime snack, Parasol caps that have reached the 'flat' stage make a memorable double-decker toasted sandwich, with a lot more flavour than the common mushroom will impart. Alternate the layers with bacon or egg, and stack them as high as decency will allow.

But enough of dallying in the grass. To the woods!

Probably the prize specimen to look out for in late summer and early autumn, is the Cep (*Boletus edulis*). The Boletus family is recognisable at a glance, because instead of gills under the cap, the spores are in tubes which open by a honeycomb of pores. There are few poisonous members of the family, and if you avoid any with reddish-coloured pores, you should be safe enough. Most are edible and good.

Cep is outstanding, because of its flavour, and also because it grows into a rather chubby specimen with lots of flesh. Worthington Smith, whose comments are generally worthy of note, says of it: 'one of the most delicious and tender objects of food ever submitted to the operation of cooking.' I have to agree. Collect the Cep when it is firm to the touch. Once soft, it has probably attracted the attention of grubs and may be full of interesting but unpalatable worm-holes.

Walk down any high street in France or Italy, in the season, generally September and October, and you will see boxes of these marvellous fungi on sale, with a scramble to buy. Cep used to be a common sight, even on the market stalls in Covent Garden, and these days you will find that many deli's stock it, bottled in oil or brine. Alas, the commercial growers of the '90s haven't been able to crack the problems of cultivation, so unless we start to emulate our continental cousins with commercial collectors in the forests of Britain, it is a do-it-yourself job. Collect your own.

They grow typically in fairly open broad-leaved woods, particularly of beech and oak. The cap is mid-brown, the colour and shape of a Bath bun. The pores are off-white, and the stem is fat and covered with a fine network of whitish, raised veins. Ceps tend to be around from August onwards in a good season.

One of the Victorian recipes suggests baking in a casserole, with onions and butter. In Italy, the caps are baked in the oven, with olive oil soaked into the pores. Young specimens are frequently added to salads, sliced and raw.

The caps can be dried and stored quite well, though of course they shrivel to fairly unrecognisable lumps. Hungary has a traditional soup recipe based on dried Cep, which turns into a very pleasant lunchtime snack. The caps are soaked in warm water, and toasted bread is added. The concoction is rubbed through a sieve, the resulting purée is seasoned and simmered with some whole caps. The Hungarians may like it like this, but to my mind the addition of some sautéed onion, basil and cream makes the result even more appetising.

Another member of the Boletus family, equally delicious on the plate, and common in woods generally, is the Bay Boletus (*Boletus badius*). So-called because of its bay brown cap, the underside has lemon yellow pores which bruise a bluish colour, and the stem is similarly coloured to the cap. Bay Boletus tastes just like Cep, with perhaps a little less flesh. Use it in the same way.

The Cauliflower Fungus (*Sparassis crispa*) is one of those outstanding creations that has you doing cartwheels (or in my case, little athletic skips) round the woods, if you find one in perfect condition. The trouble is you have to be lucky, largely because other people will have the same objective, and to some extent because the specimens are so often less than perfect. A friend of mine who manages a reserve near Guildford in Surrey says that the continental tourists are like bloodhounds on the scent when it comes to Sparassis. If it is there, they'll have it before sunrise! Sparassis grows at the foot of older pine trees. It is actually related to the bracket fungi, but is quite unlike most of them, or for that matter anything else in nature, except perhaps for a loose-textured cauliflower, hence the name.

The whole thing can be up to 30 cm across, a contorted maze of cavities and lobes. It should be creamy white and crisp throughout. What often transpires, though, is a yellowish, rather scraggy-looking job, stuck through with pine needles like a malformed porcupine. Last season, to my delight, my Surrey informant guided me to a specimen which had not been nobbled by the Germans and French, and which we filmed for the series. That was indeed as near perfect as you could wish.

To cook it, I just slice it into suitably sized pieces and gently sauté for a few minutes until tender. Another recipe suggests casseroling with milk, and on the Continent it is usually coated with beaten egg and fried. Generally, on a good sized specimen, there is too much flesh to get through in one meal, unless you have an epicurean appetite, but the Sparassis can be stored for several days by immersing the base in a bowl of water and standing somewhere cool. Alternatively, the fungus can be chopped into small pieces and dried, preferably in a similar way to the Fairy Ring caps (see page 64). Oven drying never seems to produce such good results, and ideally warm air needs to be wafting round on all sides. Stored in an air-tight jar, Sparassis reconstitutes well.

One of the highlights of my fungus-eating year is the first appearance of Honey Fungus (*Armillaria mellea*), also sometimes referred to as the Bootlace Fungus. I have seen it on sale in Italian greengrocers, with an unpronounceable name like something out of a grand opera. You have to be up early to grab any before they are sold out.

Honey Fungus is a parasite, growing on both coniferous and broad-leaved trees. It causes considerable damage to the host, and it will also feed off dead stumps and submerged roots. Not a difficult fungus to recognise, it usually grows in quite spectacular clumps. The cap is honey coloured with small darker brown fibrillar scales, and there is a ring on the stem. The gills start life rather pallid and then become a pale tawny brown, speckled with darker spots.

Do not be put off by the smell of Honey Fungus, which is rather sour when raw, and will probably have you thinking, 'This can't be right!' The moment the caps hit the pan, all will be well, and a mouth-watering aroma will elbow out the original odour. I view the moment for a gluttonous gorge on these

Top] *Sparassis crispa*

Bottom] *Armillaria mellea*

mushrooms with the same kind of anticipation that I feel for the first crop of summer strawberries. I have never suffered any ill effects, nor have the people who have gallantly shared my little snacks, though one or two have gone home looking worried! This is one of the truly delicious experiences of eating fungi, and is definitely not to be missed.

I would not recommend stewing Honey Fungus; if you choose to do so, leave the lid off the pan, to make sure any trace of acidity evaporates. For me there is only one way to cook, slicing the caps and sautéing in butter over a good heat. Cook briefly, for perhaps a minute. The flavour is strong and peppery, so no additional seasoning is wanted. Because the fungus tends to be rich, a good tip is to collect only young, firm-fleshed caps. Once they feel a bit soggy, and are starting to get dusted with white spores, leave them.

Staying with trees, there is another very much more bizarre fungus, which really is worth sampling. It is called Jew's Ear (*Auricularia auricula-judae*). One of the advantages is that it grows practically all the year round, and it is always restricted to elder trees. If you have an elder in the hedge, then the odds are that it will have some Jew's Ear on it sooner or later. It is one of the Jelly Fungi (Tremellales), which means that it can withstand very dry conditions and resuscitate once the weather turns damp again. It hangs on the branches, a sort of liver brown, rubbery ear. This is one of those collecting jobs where you really need a sharp knife, because the fruiting bodies are attached quite robustly, and unless you cut them off you will either tear the caps or play hell with your manicure.

A lot of the old books describe the culinary attributes of Jew's Ear in glowing terms, but few seem willing to offer any bright ideas on cooking. The caps are essentially rubbery, and attempting to fry or sauté will result in your having to eat something rather less than succulent. The Chinese grow something very similar on wooden palings, and probably the best way to use the caps is as they do. Part-cook them in salted water for about ten minutes, and then add them to a stir fry. It is more the texture than the taste which makes them interesting, though there is a definite flavour too. Alternatively, I have eaten the caps casseroled in milk or stock.

I am going to suggest a couple of useful little woodland numbers, for flavouring. The caps are too small to be of much use as a dish in their own right, but they do possess attractive, strong flavours, and they dry well, so they are worth standing beside the Fairy Ring Champignon on your storage rack.

There is a smallish Clitocybe, the Aniseed Agaric (*C. odora*) which I do recommend you look out for. It doesn't stand out obviously on a woodland floor, so you will need to look at the descriptions and the illustrations. However, there is little else like it, and certainly nothing poisonous.

It grows mainly in beech woods, typically in small groups on the soil, and the cap is a distinctive bluish-green, funnel-shaped like most of the family when mature, with a little umbo. Gills are paler, but essentially cap-coloured, and decurrent, and the stem is similarly coloured. The smell is the chief give-away. It is strongly aromatic, reminiscent of aniseed. The aroma survives drying well, and one or two caps added to a casserole or to a dish of more bland fungi give an interesting pep.

If you like the classic fish dish *Grillard au Fenouille* (Bass with Fennel), then an interesting alternative is to stuff the whole bass with a mixture of spinach, shallot, and Aniseed Agaric. Very tasty indeed!

In a similar vein there is a delightful small fungus called Velvet Shank (*Flammulina velutipes*). We are back searching on tree trunks again, and this is another specimen which can survive the frosts, so look out for it any time from late autumn to spring. It often grows on higher branches, so it is worth glancing upwards from time to time in your searchings. The cap is a viscid yellowish tan when damp, turning creamier in dry weather. Gills are pale or tinted cream, and the stalk, which is the most valuable identification feature, is a densely velvety chestnut brown, except immediately under the cap.

Flammulina has a strong, rather piquant flavour, and it dries well. Hang it until really leathery, then chop both caps and stems as small as possible for storage. If you are collecting and you have a few fresh caps to hand, they are well worth adding to an autumn casserole. Another tasty option is creamed Velvet Shank soup (guaranteed to interrupt the small talk at dinner). Slice and sauté a dozen or so fresh caps with shallots, till soft, then add a dessertspoon of cornflour. Stir into 500 ml of milk and 500 ml of chicken or vegetable stock

Auricularia auricula-judae

and simmer. To hell with cholesterol, let's throw in some double cream at the last minute! If, incidentally, you are coming to the conclusion that I have an obsession for cooking mushrooms with shallots, you could be right, but I am not alone, as I shall explain in the next chapter.

Poor Man's Beefsteak (*Fistulina hepatica*) is not a particular favourite of mine, but it ought to be included, because it is one of those oddities which people are bound to ask you if you have sampled. The trouble is that you have to be extremely athletic to capture it. The brackets do not appear often, but when they do, they can almost be guaranteed to be out of reach, six metres up a tree. Unless you are wearing very old jeans and have a head for heights, this can be a disadvantage.

Fistulina hepatica

The fruiting body is blood red at maturity and oozes reddish juice in wet weather. I suspect that it is this mimicry of raw meat, rather than its culinary virtues, that has given Fistulina its reputation.

However, as you are now a dedicated fungal epicure, none of this will put you off, and you are determined to add Beefsteak Fungus to your list of successes. All right, if you insist, cut it off the tree when pink, or bloody, never when dull brown. Slice and either sauté or casserole. You will come to no harm. You may in fact criticise my lack of sensitivity for a subtle flavour, but I do not think your taste buds will be over the moon. However, it is nice to have that bit of expert knowledge with which to 'wow' fellow hunters.

Settling the lie that lurid-looking fungi are unwholesome, the next offering in my Top Twenty is both lurid and tasty. Saffron Milk Cap (*Lactarius deliciosus*) is very popular on the Continent. In fact, according to C. D. Badham in his *Esculent Funguses of England*, it was exhibited in prodigious quantities in the open markets of Marseilles about a hundred years ago. He described the fungus as 'very luscious eating, full of rich gravy, with a little of the flavour of mussels'. I think the latter observation is either a case of vivid imagination, or that Mr Badham had shellfish in his larder next to his mushrooms.

The variety is good, nonetheless, though it has a very slightly bitter tang when raw; anyway, the name is surely incentive enough to experiment. The caps are quite large and fleshy, growing under or near conifers, and are a dull reddish orange colour, sometimes with a greenish tinge, and with darker and lighter rings. The cap begins life convex, and then flattens or becomes slightly funnel-shaped. Gills are cap colour, and being a Lactarius, all parts ooze an orange juice when broken.

Late autumn, and almost up until the New Year, if the weather is not too frosty, there is a real gem to be collected and eaten, the Wood Blewit (*Lepista nuda*). Old books will have this among the Tricholomas, but the boffins insisted on putting it in a separate genus some years ago. It has a cousin, the Field Blewit (*Lepista saeva*) which, as its name suggests, does not normally grow under trees. Equally delicious, but a lot less common.

The Wood Blewit has a fleshy, often rather wavy cap which starts life bluish lilac, but soon turns brownish. Gills and stem are both pale lilac although eventually, in old caps, the gills fade to buff.

The cap of the Field Blewit is a little paler than its woodland counterpart, and only the stem flushes with the blue or lilac coloration. The gills are pallid throughout life.

I collected Wood Blewits last year, in Surrey, on Boxing Day whilst attempting to walk off the effects of too much good living. The edge of one cap caught my eye, almost hidden under leaf litter and I extricated half a dozen, to wean my taste buds off turkey and mince pies. Even in mid-winter, they were still in prime condition.

Best cooked rather than eaten raw, Blewits really do make excellent eating. Years ago, in the midland shires, you would find both types on sale in the markets, but for some reason their popularity never spread. A pity, because a good Blewit will definitely knock a common mushroom off its culinary pedestal.

The traditional preparation of the fungus is similar to that of tripes, and it perhaps offers a vegetarian alternative. Remove the stems and chop them finely. Chop a couple of shallots finely and soften with a little butter in a saucepan. Add the chopped stems with a teaspoon of sage and cook gently for a minute or two. Place the caps in a saucepan, add the chopped mixture, dress with a little streaky bacon, cover with milk, and simmer for half an hour on a very low heat. Pour off the liquid and use to make a white sauce. Pour back over the caps in a serving dish. *Voilà!* According to the old recipe books, the dish should be served with mashed potato, apple sauce and croûtons.

All great fun, but the flavour of the mushrooms is well and truly smothered. If you want to savour them in their own glory, leave out the onions, the sage and the bacon. Just cook in milk, and make the white sauce, perhaps with a smidgin of lemon juice. The Blewit has a pleasantly aromatic taste which comes through nicely.

I am one short of the promised Top Twenty, and the final contestant is not an autumn specimen. It makes its appearance in the spring. St George's Mushroom (*Tricholoma gambosum*) is supposed to appear on St George's Day, April 23rd. I would not lay too much money on that. Most people agree

Lactarius deliciosus

that it tends to be around a week or so later. The mushroom appears in grassy places, and prefers chalky soils. It looks at first glance not unlike a common field mushroom turning up at the wrong time of year, but there is no ring, and the gills are the same off-white colour as the cap. It does not actually smell like a mushroom: there is a distinctly mealy aroma to the fresh caps.

The delicacy of this mushroom has been known for many a year. I even discovered a government pamphlet, published in 1947, when everybody was in the throes of rationing, which actually recommended collecting St George's Mushroom. HMSO were definitely being a little risqué. They went so far as to suggest tentative cooking tips, though with Anchor Dried Milk, powdered eggs, spuds and more spuds, these were hardly riveting. The general opinion amongst those who know these days, is that St George's Mushroom is best prepared by simmering in wine or stock.

Any of these wild mushrooms are probably best used fresh, and some, like the Boletus group, do not dry well. If you do decide to dry and store (and incidentally the dried material can be readily powdered by putting it through a blender) the best way of reconstituting is the old Chinese method. Soak in lukewarm water for five minutes, then really hot water for half an hour, as if blanching.

In some English country districts, they still pickle mushrooms, and marvellous they are too. Mix the blanched mushrooms with about twice their own weight of peeled shallots or small onions, pack into a large jar, add some pickling spice, and cover with vinegar. Simple.

Such is my short-list of delicious and wholly safe mushrooms for beginners. If, however, you think there may be some obvious omissions, read on . . .

5
Haute Cuisine

*When one eats a few truffles and drinks a glass of good wine . . .
the men become better company and the women are more
lovable.*

BRILLAT SAVARIN

For the better part of an autumn season, I had the delightful experience of wandering through the English countryside with a television camera crew, filming the location sequences for the Channel Four series of *Mushroom Magic*.

It is 10.30 on a fine balmy November morning, and I am waiting with the film crew at a remote farmhouse near Rye in Kent. We are due to meet David Chambers, Executive Head Chef at the prestigious four star Le Meridien Hotel, in London's Piccadilly. David turns up full of Londoner's patter and giving everyone the benefit of a deceptively cheeky smile. Chambers has reached the top of his professional tree. He has worked under such master chefs as Felix Muntwyler at the Portman Intercontinental, and Michel Lorain of La Côte St Jacques. He also has an unquenchable enthusiasm for cooking with wild mushrooms.

We are also to meet Matthias Luithi, an émigré from Switzerland. Matthias and his wife operate a mixed farm in Kent, but he has brought with him a Continental's passion for wild mushrooms. We set off in convoy to pine woods, courtesy of the Forestry Commission, where Matthias guarantees we will find something good!

The place breathes of fungi. They are lurking in the gloom just feet away from the track. You don't have to see them, you can *sense* that they are there. After a ten-minute trek with the camera gear we all stop and Matthias, David and I plunge into the undergrowth. Seconds later the cry goes up, like a trumpeting pheasant: *'Pieds de Mouton!'* Matthias has struck gold.

We are strictly into French titles here, the language of haute cuisine. *Pieds de Mouton*, on inspection, turn out to be what I would call Hedgehog Fungi (*Hydnum repandum*). If you are an Italian you will know them as *Steccherinos* – little hedgehogs. Here, though, they are strictly the Feet of the French Sheep! Not that I can see the similarity: the fungus is essentially creamy, mushroom coloured, but with a more wavy irregular outline to the cap. The real give-away to its identity hides underneath, because the gills are replaced by spines. There is no other fungus quite like it.

David is highly enthusiastic. *Pied de Mouton* is an ideal wild mushroom to go with rabbit or any of the whiter, lighter meats. He advocates scraping away the spines, slicing the cap and stem, and sautéing with a little butter. Several go into his collecting basket. Meanwhile, Matthias has got the bit well and truly between his teeth. From somewhere in the dark recesses of the spruce plantation, we hear him speeding after his next quarry: 'Zer are some goot *Trompettes de Mort* here!'

'Where?'

'Right here!'

We set off in convoy, in the general direction of the disembodied voice as I debate what Trumpets of Death are. The name, thankfully, turns out to be deceptive. Matthias has come across one of his 'hot favourites' in this particular forest, the Horn of Plenty (*Craterellus cornucopoides*). It is also one of my particular delights, so the three of us are prancing around like kids at a birthday party.

These are rather unusual fungi, more closely related to Brackets than Agarics. Instead of gills, the outside of the trumpet-shaped cap is lined with blunt, forked ridges. The whole specimen is grey, darker on top and paler, more ash-toned, on the ridged underside where the spores are carried. We pick as many as will decently go into the basket. Matthias is a great believer in cutting the stems, not pulling them up. He regards this as an important measure in conservation of the stocks.

David Chambers is crowing about the find. He uses *Trompette de Mort* as often as he can get hold of fresh supplies. The subtle flavour, he believes, provides the ideal complement to fish.

Already the daylight is fading and the pace intensifies. We find a good patch

Cantharellus cibarius

of the famous Chanterelle (*Cantharellus cibarius*), which sometimes has the local French name of *La Girolle*. These are, of course, the classic fungi of France and a delightful meal they make.

The fungus is of similar construction to the *Trompette de Mort*, though the cap starts life dome-shaped and only becomes funnel-like as it matures. The whole thing is a delicious apricot yellow, with a faintly fruity aroma and a peppery aftertaste on the tip of the tongue.

There is only one species with which *C. cibarius* can be confused, the False Chanterelle (*Hygrophoropsis aurantiaca*). This, though, has proper plate-like gills under the cap, not ridges. It is harmless, merely having a rather off-putting acrid flavour, so the worst that can happen if you include a cap or two in your dish, is that you will be forced to spit out a rather unpalatable mouthful.

Top] *Hydnum repandum*   [83]

Bottom] *Craterellus cornucopoides*

We also find a third member of this group of fungi, which I learn is known in high culinary circles as *Chanterelle Grise*. It has no common English name and its scientific title is enough to generate a mild headache, *Cantharellus infundibuliformis*. It is not dissimilar to the true Chanterelle, but is generally more delicately built with a thinner, longer stem. This and the underside of the cap are apricot yellow, but the upper cap surface is a dingy brown, not grey as the French name implies.

By mid-afternoon, we are all rather chilly and the daylight is virtually gone, so the hunt is called off. David is happy with his day's 'catch' and heads back to Le Meridien. The crew sets off for a tea-shop that someone says does terrific scones and clotted cream.

Shortly after that day in the Kentish forests, I visited David Chambers in his kitchen at Le Meridien and watched him preparing some truly superb dishes, in which fungi of the kind we had been collecting played a prominent part.

Just to whet my appetite, and to keep me from drooling over subsequent dishes which were destined for 'upstairs' at £20 per helping, he knocked up a little pasta for me to try. Like any master of his profession, David works with a marvellous fluidity and economy of movement. The heat from the gas plates is the first and most shocking experience. Nothing in a domestic kitchen even comes close to it. You suspect that your eyeballs are turning to a nice crisp brown, and your breath is taken away. David has become immune, shrugging off the assault with a wipe of perspiration.

He is a delight to watch, using the tips of his fingers to flick little dabs of butter into a skillet, and swirling slices of wild mushroom – Chanterelles, Ceps, *Pieds de Mouton* – for only a few sizzling seconds before drawing them off the heat. For my taster he added chopped shallots and tomato, a hint of basil and a dash of cream, all tossed with the tagliatelle. He describes such a dish as simple, but devouring it before the camera, with a kitchen spoon and considerable lack of finesse, I thought it was just wonderful, a subtle blend of flavours, textures and colours.

The kitchen table, and not the forest floor, is the place to be selective about which specimens to retain and which to discard. As often as not you will find yourself gathering your Chanterelles or Ceps without too much concern for the finer points of each specimen. Once back to base, discard any but fresh, healthy-looking specimens.

They do not have to be in their first flush of youth, but anything which is shrivelled, discoloured, soggy or overly smelly should go straight into the dustbin, as should any specimens with signs that maggots have taken up residence within.

Remember, though, that some wild mushrooms will not have the 'feel' of the familiar varieties. Boleti may seem spongy, and Chanterelles have a brittle elastic texture.

One of the little practical tips that makes a few hours in the company of a chef like David Chambers so valuable concerns washing the fungi. He recommends not washing anything until immediately before you cook it. Leave the caps dirty and dry until the last minute. My instinct would be to wash the whole specimen, but no, David's point is that this will often leave bits of dirt and grit lurking in awkward corners. Cut away the base of the stem and any damaged bits, slice the caps and stems, then rinse in a colander and everything comes out clean and grit-free. The slices can be dried gently on a tea-towel before cooking. Very few wild mushrooms need peeling, incidentally. It spoils the appearance and does nothing to improve the edibility.

David Chambers is fortunate enough to have wild mushrooms coming into Le Meridien's kitchen twice a week almost throughout the year. He regularly imports from abroad as well as obtaining home-collected material from Matthias Luithi. For most of us, however, storage for a few days is going to be desirable.

Invariably, you seem to collect far more than can possibly be eaten at a sitting, and the last thing you want to do is to throw the surplus in the dustbin. Most fungi will keep for a day or two in the fridge. Make sure that the specimens are dry, and place them in a polythene tub covered with tinfoil. Always check and wash them before using. Little wrigglers will not be deterred by the chilling of a fridge.

David is a great advocate of putting the right fungi with each dish. His idea of the perfect appetiser at a dinner party is a green salad, topped with warm

Still life of wild mushrooms delivered to Le Meridien

*Top left] With David Chambers in the kitchens
of Le Meridien, Piccadilly*

Top right] David Chambers at work . . .

*Bottom] . . . transforming wild mushrooms into perfectly presented
and delicious dishes*

goose liver and decorated with sliced Cep. The Cep is there not just for its flavour, but for texture too. He seems always to be keen on starting with a little chopped shallot. It will, he insists, bring out the flavour of the mushrooms. All is arranged perfectly. So much of the skill of a master chef lies in the look of a finished dish. The salad, topped with its goose liver, is central on the plate and the Cep slices are arranged fanwise around the edge. All the cooked ingredients are heated through with great speed.

To complement a fish dish, like *Filet de Sole*, David selects *Trompettes de Mort* cooked quickly with a little shallot, and he adds mussels to the plate, sautéed with *Pieds de Mouton* to give them a distinctively earthy flavour. The fillets are undercooked, almost in seconds rather than minutes, and are arranged in a star pattern. Between each one the black of the *Trompettes* contrasts dramatically with the pure white of the fish. As the dish comes together, the *Pieds de Mouton* and mussel mixture goes in the centre, and a lobster butter sauce is poured around the main elements.

The result is as much a work of art as a culinary masterpiece. Michel Lorain has taught David Chambers to marry up ingredients, rather than just putting a dish together for the sake of it. Look at the material, consider its flavour, texture and appearance, and decide what it can go with.

Red meats like steak or venison almost beg, Chambers believes, for Chanterelles. The wild mushrooms go into the saucepan to sauté with the inevitable shallots. Three little venison steaks are cooked at lightning speed and arranged with the inevitable symmetry. A potato basket on top takes a crèche of baby vegetables. Sauce from venison bones and wine marinade is drifted artistically around, deep red and gamy. A little chopped herb flutters over the mushrooms. He revels in fresh herbs.

You can tell he is in love with all these things. Occasionally he will mutter terms of endearment: 'Beautiful mushrooms! Magnificent *Pieds de Mouton*!' His south London French has an endearing quality.

Chambers insists that he doesn't 'hang his hat on any one sign', merely that he has a 'feel' for food. It is quite clear though that modesty is talking. He understands and has a sympathy for wild mushrooms, in the manner of a true Continental chef. He admits to cooking mushrooms at home, and one of the delights of his recipes is that you can actually practise them in your own kitchen. It is all in the blend of materials, the presentation and the speed of working.

David also admits, and it is a point worth remembering, that although Matthias often brings in a wide assortment of fresh specimens, he will only utilise those which he is familiar with and which he has eaten with confidence.

Mushrooms are not yet a sought-after ingredient in British cuisine. It is more a case of people ordering the sole and when it arrives at table, saying, 'Oh look, wild mushrooms, what a lovely idea!'

Many recipes rely on what can be created from the market, so Chambers has been endeavouring to use as much wild mushroom as he can to make the public aware of what, at the right time of year, they can go out and find for themselves. Many of the Chanterelles he uses are British born and bred. They come down from the pine forests of Scotland. Ironically, they used often to go from Scotland to France, and thence to Britain. The Scots, not surprisingly, have stopped the practice and these days they market genuine tartan Chanterelles straight to London!

To obtain the full experience of wild mushroom eating, though, you must still cross to the Continent. There they view wild mushrooms with true reverence. At weekends during 'the season' in France and Italy and no doubt a lot of other places as well, cars parked by the verge, boot lids open, are a familiar sight on country roads. In Britain, the owners would be picnicking. On the Continent, they are toting their mushroom baskets and scurrying through the woods like demented squirrels. Chanterelles, Ceps, Trompettes, Russulas are all fair game.

In fact, the woods are probably over-cropped. They say that if you want to find wild mushrooms growing in France it is no good looking on a Monday!

There tend to be two high spots in the mushroom year, the morel crop in springtime, and the emergence of the truffles in October. If, however, you go out looking for the latter, you are more likely than not to come back empty-handed. Truffles are not at all easy to find without special assistance in the shape of a trained animal.

Poodles were the traditional truffle hounds in France, though pigs have also

Tuber aestivum

been put to work rooting them out. Pigs are poor contenders, though, because they find it difficult to appreciate the importance of retrieving without eating, and the owner runs a serious risk of losing fingers in trying to part his truffle-troving porker from the quarry.

The black truffle, found largely in the Périgord region of France, and not unlike our summer truffle (*Tuber aestivum*), lies buried a few centimetres below the soil surface, and has the appearance of an overcooked chestnut with warts.

The highly distinctive smell of truffles, attributable to a chemical, dio-mythol sulphate, is designed to procure their effective dispersal around the countryside. The odour is an irresistible attraction to a number of animals, and the spores passed unscathed through to the creatures' nether regions, whence they are liberated far and wide.

It is, of course, the heady aroma which gives the truffles their culinary mystique. It is a smell which will have you either in ecstasy or holding your nose. There is no happy medium, though it is perhaps an acquired taste. To describe the aroma of truffles is impossible. It is pungent, earthy, garlicky, and yet none of those adjectives is truly accurate. It is one of those experiences you have to savour at first hand.

In any event, this remarkable odour earns the French truffle hunter who can bear to part with his prizes up to £400 per pound (£880 per kilo). Not surprisingly, the truffles are known as 'black diamonds' and 'black gold' in the Paris markets.

To witness the real cult of truffle eating, though, you have to go to northern Italy. The Langhe province of Piemonte nestling under the Alps in the northwest, is the home of the famed white truffles (*Tuber magnatum*). These aromatic delicacies grow under plantations of poplar and oak which dot the Tintoretto landscape of gentle valleys and hilltop villages. The region is damp and cool for much of the year, and in autumn the mornings are cocooned in soft mists that hug the valley floors and keep the soil moist.

To the north Italian, mushrooms are near to being a religion. They even boast mushroom museums at Boves and Pinorelo. In Cuneo there are factories drying, canning and preserving mushrooms to sell all over the world.

Autumn sees the gathering of truffle aficionados from every continent, for the Truffle Festival in the medieval town of Alba. There, for six weeks from late September to early November, the world revolves around the magical truffles, the *tartufi*. To the south, in Umbria, they collect black truffles, but these are considered greatly inferior in flavour. They are also a lot more common, which I suspect may have something to do with the esteem for the Alba truffle. Alba, I discovered, does not mean *white* as an English speaker might believe but *dawn*, which makes the name seem even prettier.

For a purist, the only way to consume the white truffle is on the day of its capture, but for the less fastidious a whole industry is geared to marketing these extraordinary objects. Truffles are dried, pickled, shredded, and used to flavour pâté and olive oil. You can even buy plastic truffles for the mantelpiece, truffle sweatshirts and truffle tea towels. The smell of the truffles soaks relentlessly into your nostrils as you walk down the main shopping street, the Via Vittoria Emanuele.

The high spot of the business side of things comes in the open truffle market. Ostensibly, this is where all the wheeling and dealing is done, but much of the business is, in truth, carried on in discreet meetings of buyers and sellers in the dawn light at private country rendezvous. The market is more of interest for the restaurateurs and shopkeepers.

Slowly on Saturday morning, there gathers a congregation of dealers and of *trifoli*, the truffle hunters. Generally these are men of unfathomable years, possessed of gnarled, earth-begrimed hands and the complexions of walnut chopping blocks. Each bears his booty coyly concealed in a paper bag or a handkerchief that has seen better days, and which he clutches like a hoard of prized gob-stoppers.

The buyers are recognisable by their marginally more affluent appearance, and the absence of paper bags. Nothing much seems to happen for a long time. There is a good deal of macho Italian sizing-up. Everyone mingles in a rather casual, off-hand manner, and there is much chat with shrugging of shoulders and shaking of heads. Beneath all this indifference, though, is a strong sense of anticipation. Specimens are weighed minutely to several decimal places under watchful eyes and then, without warning, a wad of money of awesome proportions may appear. Italian finances seem to be arrived at by taking a figure and adding noughts, on occasions somewhat vaguely, which makes the mathematics of even the simplest transaction rather startling. Several million lire are peeled off the roll in crumpled bank notes, followed by a smooth transfer of goods, a shake of hands, and the deal is done.

The taste of the truffle is too strong on its own, so it is used in very small quantities as a flavouring for other dishes. Just as well, because the prices are truly astronomical. On the day I visited the Alba market, I saw a single specimen weighing in at about half a kilo and looking like a cross between a knobbly potato and a Jerusalem artichoke, change hands for the equivalent of nearly £800.

Many of the smaller truffles are consumed locally in the superb restaurants and *alberghi* of the region, but some of the better specimens find their way as far afield as Berlin, New York and Los Angeles. President Reagan had a weakness for white truffles, and during his administration they frequently turned up at Washington state banquets, presumably having earned an impressive number of dollars en route from the woods of Piemonte.

The *trifoli* equip their hounds with home-made wire muzzles. Ostensibly, these prevent the animals from eating their quarry. Apparently almost all will succumb to temptation if they feel they can get away with it. There is, however, a more dire reason for the muzzling. *Tartufi* are big business for the local hunters and there is intense competition. A *trifolau*, possessed of a hound with a good nose, can earn up to £25,000 in a season, and such are the stakes that it is not unknown for a 'hot' truffle-snuffler to be nobbled by envious rival owners. Several dogs each season fall victim to poisoned bait. The hunters generally frown on poisoning as extremely unsporting behaviour, because they become attached to their dogs and it takes several years to train a good animal. Often the hunting is carried out under cover of night and with considerable stealth. The *trifoli* insist that the odour of the truffles is stronger in the damp night air, but everyone knows it is more because they want to visit their choice locations unobserved.

When I joined a truffle hunt, several dogs emerged from the impossible confines of a small car boot, apparently none the worse, and high-tailed it for the woods. Clearly they knew what they were after. The elderly *trifoli*, armed with walking sticks, briar pipes and, mysteriously, lumps of stale bread, set off at a more leisurely pace. The dogs best suited to the job, I was told, are mongrels, though looking at the squad we had with us, I suspect that many could claim dalliance by a labrador or a pointer somewhere in their chequered ancestry. Bitches make the best truffle hounds, apparently less likely to be distracted, but the dogs are not fed for a day or two before the hunt so as to focus their attentions more firmly on the job in hand.

Once in the woods, the dogs began quartering for scent and eventually one narrowed down the area of search and started frantically scrabbling at a patch of leaf litter. The *trifolau* to whom the beast belonged was there beside it with startling alacrity, muttering words of encouragement, and eventually retrieving a rather grimy specimen. The dog, by now extremely hungry and with its

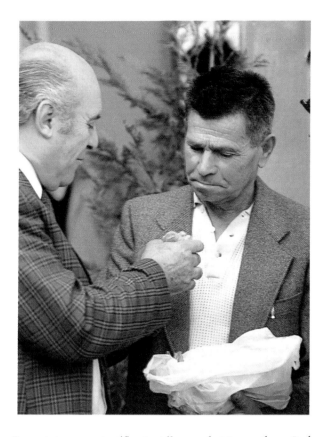

Bargaining over truffles in Alba market in northern Italy

juices in full flow, was persuaded to hand over the prize in exchange for a small lump of bread!

The proof of the truffling is, of course, in the eating and to this end the Festival is marked by a phenomenon known as the *Pranzo Speciale*. The term translates, quite simply, as a binge of momentous proportions.

At least an afternoon, but to be on the safe side a full twenty-four hours, needs to be set aside for recuperation from this experience, and ideally several weeks of training *à la table* should be pursued. An athletically fit digestive system is a must.

Italian trifolau *and his hound*   [95]

I landed up in Feisoglio, a small mountain village in the main street of which is La Ristorante Renato, an unprepossessing block house. Its appearance is deceptive. Through the door an attractive restaurant beckons. I shared my initiation into the *Pranzo Speciale* with charming fellow gourmet and mentor, Elena. Blessed, like most north Italian girls, with a lissom, startlingly leggy figure, Elena was to steer me through the finer points of feeding Piemonte-style. Bib tucked in, I eyed the carte in wary anticipation: less a menu than an outline synopsis. Fourteen courses . . . or was it fifteen? Determined not to let the home team down, I braced myself.

Renato, the *padrone*, swirled in with the first of an immodest number of antipasti. This was a gentle little starter, a salad of valerian and mushroom dressed with oil and lemon. Renato's apron pockets concealed the *pièce de résistance*, a fresh white truffle. Wielding a special instrument like a cheese parer, *il mandolino*, he began his magic. Slivers of *tartufo* fluttered, wafer-thin, across my plate like dreamy delicate snowflakes.

Renato is a restaurateur by pedigree. He runs a family business begun by his great-grandfather. His forte lies in the preparation of the traditional dishes of Piemonte, each based on the use of truffles and other mushrooms like *porcini*, the Italian version of the Cep. He prides himself on about a hundred different recipes, using mushrooms each with its own distinctive flavour.

Opening the restaurant at Easter, he makes good use of the spring varieties. The fun begins with San Giorgio mushrooms, an irony considering that their name and claim to fame comes from England, where they are practically unheard of. Morels he waves away disparagingly as second class fare and not for the more discerning spring gourmet. You can tell where his loyalties lie. Standing in his *cucina*, surrounded by gleaming pots and pans and the all-pervading aroma of truffles, and trying to keep my brain cells in pace with Renato's quick-fire Piemonte chat (do they all talk this fast?) was definitely an all-Italian experience.

My apprehension heightened for a moment when he mentioned casually that the average Sunday lunch menu includes a minimum of twenty courses. What day was this? Had I misread the menu? Could I still count? Thankfully, we were in for the sissy version only. With an interesting brand of conversation, rather more fluent on my companion's part than mine, and being regularly lubricated by a sublime locally bottled Dolcetto, hand-in-hand with a fine Barolo, we were off!

Several hours and innumerable *antipasti* later, with the first of the main courses still under Renato's ministering hand in the *cucina*, and all liberally dusted with flakes of truffle, I was fading fast.

Bearing in mind that each of these courses consisted of what I would regard as a small meal in itself – morsels of fish, ham, cheese, mushroom, resting all too frequently on a *de rigueur* plateau of tagliatelli or vermicelli, I think I did rather well to last as long as I did.

Elena, on the other hand, was evidently either programmed from birth or in heavy training for the job. Her capacity to demolish pasta belied that sylph-like figure. She presented the appetite of an undernourished stevedore.

By the time we had reached the gastronomic summit and were sliding down towards the *formaggi* and *dolce*, I was past caring. I dimly recall the lady wooing me towards attacking a mountainous portion of cheesecake, but all in vain. The grappa, the national Italian liqueur which to my uncultured palate has the taste and symptoms of diesel oil, and which conventionally rounds off these little adventures, also neatly finished me.

So, you demand an answer. Is the white truffle truly an aphrodisiac? I wouldn't know. You will have to find out for yourself!

6

The Mushroom Industry

According to the latest estimates, the citizens of the United Kingdom munch their way through £350,000,000 worth of mushrooms a year which, at something around £1 per lb (£2.20 per kilo), is big business. In fact, in horticultural terms it is the biggest. According to figures published in 1988 mushrooms are the most valuable horticultural crop produced in the UK. We spend more on mushrooms than baked beans and the demand is rising. Yet our conservatism about the kind of mushrooms we eat is lamentable.

Gone are the days when the only option by way of a commercially available mushroom was *Agaricus bisporus*, frequently dismembered in its infancy as a neat and well-nigh tasteless button. Yet do we take advantage of modern methods that permit such delights as Oyster Mushroom to appear on the supermarket shelves? Sadly, we have a lot of catching up to do, before we join the enlightened ranks of mycophiles on the Continent. In most parts of the country, it is still almost impossible even to find 'flats' in the local supermarkets, though they alone possess any real flavour. To obtain Brown Caps, Oyster Caps, Shitake or any of the other less familiar cultivated species is a rare treat.

The statistics speak for themselves. 99% of all mushrooms sold commercially are white *A. bisporus*, and of those, up to 80% of the total crop are either buttons or closed cups. Supermarkets and processors are interested in little that has grown beyond the button stage. The 20% or so of mushrooms grown on to become open cups or flats are generally cultivated on specialist farms geared to their production.

Of the remaining 1% of mushrooms grown commercially, most are Brown Caps, a sub-species of *A. bisporus*, and the tiny fraction remaining represents

Agaricus bisporus

the truly innovative material like Shitake and Oyster Cap.

It is not entirely the fault of our timid palates. Unusual species, commercially grown here, are still considered uneconomical to produce. According to one of the vegetable produce buyers for Marks and Spencer, 'Mrs Average British Housewife' is unwilling to spend £1.50 for fifty grams of something that, to her, does not look too appetising.

Attitudes to foodstuffs in general are changing fast, however, and we are becoming much more venturesome in our choice of fruit and vegetables. Not so long ago, the avocado pear was a huge novelty regarded as an acquired taste by all but the enlightened few. Now, my six-year-old daughter attacks avocados with the same nonchalance and speed that she applies to demolishing jelly babies.

Several factors have influenced this increased adventurousness in our tastebuds, not least the spread of Chinese restaurants and take-aways. The Chinese were amongst the pioneers in the use of the exotic and the unusual in the kitchen. We have also become more catholic in our acceptance of spices and unfamiliar flavours. We have generally grown up not a little since the dark days of post-war rationing, when I distinctly remember the thrill of my own first foray into the unknown – the taste of a fresh banana!

So, the mushroom-growing industry is gearing itself slowly but surely to meet new demands from us, the consumers. Or at least it is gearing itself to those of us who still *want* to buy our mushrooms over the counter, after experiencing the delights of pick-your-own forays to the countryside!

Some supermarkets are apparently reintroducing Oyster Caps and Shitake, with new packaging giving more 'eye appeal', and they are coupling the sales drive with information and recipes.

I wonder how many people are familiar with Shitake? No, it is not a Japanese martial art, although it does have a strong popular following in the Far East.

Bill Slee and Alistair Campbell are heavily into Shitake, down in the depths of the West Country. Newton Abbot may shortly become famous for more than the joys of racing over the jumps and Devonshire clotted cream, because just away from the town, at the Seale Hayne Agricultural College, they are pioneering research into the possibilities of growing the Shitake mushroom on a commercial scale in Britain, on timber.

In part, the interest has been stimulated by the need to find alternative productive enterprises for woodlands, which make the best use of the land both economically and environmentally. The West Country possesses acres of underexploited woodland, particularly oak.

Once carefully coppiced, it is now an abandoned legacy of bygone industries manufacturing charcoal and tannins. Those same woodlands lie disused and under threat from the more commercially popular plantation of conifers. Shitake, the name given to various strains of *Lentinus edodes*, is one of the few types of commercially proven mushrooms which grow on wood.

Existing commercial growers operate indoors. They cultivate the spawn in a sawdust base, with a cocktail of chemical additives. Slee and Campbell argue that the product which emerges is inferior. They believe that the only way to grow Shitake so that the full 'wild' flavour is achieved is to grow it on logs out of doors. The pioneer 'farm' is in fact in an oak wood behind Bill Slee's cottage.

The two men work in tandem. Slee organises the field trials, whilst Alistair Campbell works in the laboratory. Experimentation with different varieties is essential. There are more than a hundred strains of Japanese Shitake, some of which will probably grow better and faster than others in our climate and, more particularly, on our available trees.

The Shitake spawn is inoculated into oak logs, in small dowels or plugs placed into drill holes which are then sealed with wax to prevent the intrusion of unwanted pests or competitive strains of 'weed' fungi, and is allowed to spread through the timber stacked in the open. The process takes a year to eighteen months. The log is then plunged into cold water for two days, enough to give the fungus the idea that things have gone seriously wrong in its world.

The knack of any commercial mushroom-growing programme is to get the mycelium to produce fruiting bodies on demand, rather than when the activity comes naturally. Shitake will tend to produce its fruits when it 'thinks' that its future well-being is in jeopardy. The name of the survival game in the world of fungi is to spread spores before it is too late. In nature, that situation arises when the temperature begins to drop in the autumn.

There are, needless to say, all sorts of incidental problems to overcome. Rogue fungi can infest the wood, and set up in competition with the Shitake. Slugs and snails will go into concerted attack unless dissuaded. There are decisions to be made about the positioning of the logs on which the mycelium grows. Do you stack them in piles, set them up like a stockade, or prop them together like a wigwam? How far apart must they be spaced? Should they be covered?

These are not trivial considerations. They will have a considerable influence on the way the mushroom grows. Whether or not it develops into an attractive shape is an important factor in deciding its commercial viability. All

. . . and, eighteen months later, the mouth-watering Shitake

are practical decisions which are being assessed at Seale Hayne.

Outside of the Far East, Shitake is grown extensively in the United States, but Campbell and Slee are convinced that setting up farms *au naturel* can be a viable enterprise in Britain.

A log will remain good as a source of food for the mycelium for up to six years, though with a steadily diminishing crop return. So far, at best, they have managed to crop a single log of a kilo of mushrooms in a season.

In Japan, Shitake is treated almost reverentially: a kind of fungal ginseng. It is said to reduce blood pressure, stimulate the immune system, and . . . yes,

Oak logs inoculated with
Shitake spawn . . .

[103]

you've guessed, some regard it as an aphrodisiac!

The mushroom has more body than *Agaricus bisporus* when cooked, but what does it taste like? Bill Slee's eyes go a little misty on this topic. It is, he suggests, meaty and smoky with a hint of garlic. The proof of his assessment can be savoured to a degree, in some supermarkets, though generally not as yet in the provinces. But what is on sale is a commercial item, grown indoors on sawdust and, Slee insists, 'a poorer quality product'. They aim to breed 'em strong down in glorious Devon.

Many of the larger mushroom growers invest considerable budgets in research to find new and more successful types of spawn, but by and large the effort is still directed towards good old *A. bisporus*.

One of the biggest growers in the country is Chesswood, at Thakeham in West Sussex. Founded in 1882 by an enterprising fruit grower called Arthur Linfield, its annual production is now in excess of 120,000 tonnes.

For a commercial grower of common mushrooms, the knack is much as with Shitake: to make a plant which has natural inclinations to offer up fruiting bodies once a year, produce a 365 day crop. It is also to find the right strain to give you the kind of mushroom you want. The strains used for 'button' production are different from those employed to yield 'flats'. Actually growing the spawn is far from simple.

Most major growers also need to run a separate farming enterprise which generates the compost needed to grow the mushroom crop. It is usually based on wheat straw. Back in the old days this was mixed with horse manure. Nowadays, horses and their droppings are not as common as in Arthur Linfield's time, so alternative sources of manure have to be utilised.

In Chesswood's case that enterprise is pigs, nearly 10,000 of them, all doing their gallant best to produce the vital ingredients for a thousand tons of compost which the mushrooms eat their saprophytic way through each and every week. It takes a month to prepare the compost, including a week for pasteurisation. The mixture is dampened, then formed into long stacks about two metres square in profile and up to fifty metres long, and for three weeks the compost must be turned regularly.

Needless to say, with that quantity of material to be handled, the process is heavily mechanised and vast machines trundle down the stacks mixing the material.

The object is to encourage the microbes in the compost to use up the easily available foods, leaving the tougher materials on which the mushrooms can feed without competition. At the end of the month-long process, a completely homogenised sterile compost is ready for the mushroom spawn.

'Spawn' is a commercially coined term for mushroom mycelium inoculated into moist sterilised grain. By using spawn rather than spores, the fungal material is easier to handle and can be distributed evenly through the compost. The quality of the spawn is, of course, vital to successful propagation. It is prepared under clinical laboratory conditions and supplied to the grower in sealed containers.

Once the compost has been inoculated and colonised, it is covered by a 'casing' of fresh peat and chalk. At this stage the compost is usually contained in long wooden trays, stacked in tiers down the length of the mushroom sheds. To encourage the colonisation, the temperature is kept to about 25°C, with a high level of carbon dioxide. The process usually takes about a fortnight and it may involve chilling the compost beds because the mycelium activity can quickly build up considerable heat. Why the peat and chalk? To keep the 'spawn run', as the developed mycelium is called, in just the right condition to produce fruiting bodies. The moisture, warmth, and carbon dioxide in the compost are all critical.

To encourage the mushrooms to develop, the air temperature is controlled to between 16°C and 20°C and the relative humidity is held at between 85% and 95%.

The carbon dioxide level is reduced by 'ventilating'. The moisture content in the compost is still critical. If these things are just right the mycelium is encouraged towards the surface of the casing and the mushrooms start to form. At one time, it was all down to the skill and intuition of the man on the ground. These days, the individual skills are still very much needed, but mushroom farming has gone high-tech, and in many units computers control the day-to-day environment.

It takes about seven to ten days for the first little white pinheads to appear, and these are big enough to crop in about the same length of time again. From then on, mushrooms are produced in 'flushes' at seven to ten day intervals, each flush being picked over a three or four day period.

One of the lesser known facts of the mushroom industry is that the caps continue to grow after they have been picked. The stems grow longer, the veils tear, and closed buttons can open out. So knowing just when to pick to provide the customer, who is putting the mushrooms in the shopping basket, the correct stage of growth, is a skilled job. Mushrooms also bruise easily and if they are handled anything less than gently, they discolour and lose their value as well as deteriorating faster.

Most of the crop is picked in the first three weeks, but harvesting can go on for about six weeks with steadily diminishing yields. In terms of yield, a 4000 square foot (370 square metres) growing unit is reckoned to produce about 20,000 lbs (9000 kilos) of mushrooms per cycle. Enough to cope with a few fried breakfasts.

At the other end of the commercial scale, mushrooms are grown on small-holdings up and down the country. Some have been discovered in very odd places indeed. A mushroom farm even found its way into the heart of London and buttons were soon a-sprouting under railway arches rented from British Rail. Mushroom compost was ferried in to the capital, and it is said that, when it had done its work, dustmen were bribed to take it away again!

Mushrooms are very nutritious, even though much of their weight is made up by water. They contain more protein than many other vegetables, have no cholesterol and are low in calories and fat. During his explorations in HMS *Beagle*, Charles Darwin came across an isolated tribe living in Tierra del Fuego in the extreme south of the American continent, who were using a species of fungus as a staple diet. It grows on evergreen beech trees throughout the year. Darwin named it *Cyttaria Darwinii*.

Yet in spite of all the benefits, farms producing Oyster Caps and other such delights come and go for lack of business. Oyster Caps (*Pleurotus ostreatus*) are traditionally grown on dead logs, though the mycelium will produce fruiting bodies on a range of materials from tree stumps to tea leaves! One of the leading fungal spawn laboratories, Darlington's in Sussex, offer an Oyster

Cap kit which they will send through the post for a modest fee.

Each pack contains enough spawn to inoculate 100 kilogrammes of wood, so if you live in the south east with a large garden wrecked after the great storm of 1986, here is an opportunity to do-it-yourself. Contact Darmycel Ltd, Station Road, Rustington, West Sussex BN16 3RD.

You can also purchase kits at any reputable garden centre from which to grow common mushrooms in the kitchen cupboard, and there are now kits available from which you can also inoculate a garden lawn with mushroom spawn.

We have no excuse!

There are, of course, many other sides to the commercial value of fungi. During the 1930s an American researcher from the Michigan Academy of Science, E. H. Lucas, visited a small mountain village in Bohemia. Reports had filtered through that lumberjacks in the area had implicit faith in the cancer-retarding properties of a mushroom which turned out to be the Cep (*Boletus edulis*). Lucas returned to the United States and investigated the claims at the Sloan Kettering Institute for Cancer Research, using mice infected with cancerous tumours.

Although at the time the results were hailed as a major breakthrough in cancer-retardation therapy, they are now considered to be inconclusive. It is also impossible under present techniques either to grow Cep in culture, or to manufacture the chemicals involved. Biotechnology is also exploring ways of using fungi to attack the problem of rheumatoid arthritis. It is believed that the process which triggers the disease can be interfered with using chemical compounds extracted from lichens, which are symbiotic associations of fungi and algae.

At some time in the future, who knows, there may be a discovery as revolutionary as penicillin.

The International Mycological Institute prides itself on the ledgers in which are hand-written every culture submitted to them for safe-keeping. The yearbook for 1947 contains a memorable entry. A certain A. Fleming submitted a strain of mould called *Penicillium notatum* . . . Today that same strain is the source of a multi-million pound industry which has probably saved the lives of millions of people.

[107]

7

Poisonous Fungi

On his shelf I'll put out surely basketfuls of old toadstools
All dried up and leathery, tainted ones and poisonous
Let him eat them greedily, meet his end right speedily.

FOLK SONG: MOUSSORGSKY

The apprehension of the average person about the dangers inherent in mushrooms and toadstools is probably overstated. The risks receive notoriety because, occasionally, people who dabble with fungi seem hell-bent on breaking the normal rules of common sense in the countryside. The object of this chapter is not to frighten anyone, but merely to explain the extent of the different types of poisoning and how to avoid coming to grief if you are tempted to pick and eat wild mushrooms. Additionally, it offers a practical summary of the all-important first aid know-how, should you or anyone with you fall inadvertent victim to fungal poisoning.

At risk of becoming boringly repetitive, the number of *lethally* poisonous fungi in the British Isles can be counted on the fingers of both hands and, furthermore, because many of the Amanitas probably rely on a mycorrhizal association with specific host trees, most of the lethally poisonous mushrooms are quite uncommon.

On the bottom line the point is that this chapter will be irrelevant, if the simple rules of the game are obeyed. Here is a fair illustration of how not to do it, an incident that actually took place, though with the names of the *dramatis personae* changed.

In the autumn of 1980 Chris took his girlfriend Jane to the New Forest for a weekend. Out walking on the Saturday they picked what he later described as a 'large mushroom'. Neither Chris nor Jane could identify it, yet that evening Chris ate a small piece raw 'just to see if it was OK'.

He suffered no obvious ill-effects, so he assumed it was safe to eat and, still without identifying it properly, included the rest of the mushroom in Sunday's cooked breakfast. Twelve hours later, having returned home and by now suffering from severe cramps, vomiting and diarrhoea, he took himself along to the local hospital where he was diagnosed to be suffering from food poisoning. Back at home bouts of vomiting and diarrhoea continued, and in the next three days Chris lost seven kilos. Jane, having gone her own way after the weekend, was admitted to hospital suffering from similar symptoms and acute dehydration.

Inexplicably, Chris sought no further medical advice or treatment. Instead, he made his will and went to friends thinking he was about to expire.

Fortunately he recovered, but in consequence he retains a deep-seated phobia about wild mushrooms. Jane predictably takes the same view. Now he never eats fungi 'unless they come out of a supermarket wrapper.' Yet Chris broke practically every rule in the book and really only had himself to blame.

Nature dictates far more brutal laws in the countryside than our cosy cocooned world of technology gears us to expect. Most of us are urban creatures whether we like it or not. Even if we live in the country, we are no longer directly dependent upon it for our well-being in the way that our ancestors were. Danger and death are, in reality, everyday matters in the wild and if we venture into what has become an alien world we must abide by its rules.

The irony of Chris's situation is that he would probably no more have entertained the prospect of collecting a basketful of strange berries from the hedgerow and eating them, than of jumping in front of a train. Yet he was willing to pick an unfamiliar plant in the woods and eat it as if he were playing gastronomic Russian roulette.

Eating wild fungi is no more, and probably rather less, hazardous than collecting blackberries or wild strawberries. It needs only to be treated with caution and above all good sense. Many of the reported deaths from eating wild mushrooms could so easily have been avoided, had the victim not merely assumed that the variety was edible without making the proper checks.

It is also important to realise that not everyone will be affected in the same way. Whereas one person can eat a particular specimen and suffer no ill-effects, another may experience acute nausea or tummy ache. With many fungi, the expression 'poisonous' is applied in a broad sense. It does not necessarily mean something which harms or kills for certain.

A definition of the effect might be: 'departure from the normal state of health when a small portion of the material is eaten by a person susceptible to its effects.' In other words, some kinds of plant poisoning verge on causing allergic reactions.

The symptoms experienced by Chris and Jane are fairly typical of the early stages of illness resulting from plant poisons generally, not just those that stem from eating unwholesome fungi. The sickness and diarrhoea are usually accompanied by stomach ache, and in most cases represent the first real distress of the victim. Sometimes, but by no means always, there is an immediate warning of something amiss. The food may taste bitter or acrid, or it may produce a burning sensation in the mouth and throat. This alerts the victim to spit out whatever they are about to swallow. These symptoms are usually short-lived and very localised.

There is then, always, a lapse of time between eating the material and the showing of any further symptoms. It is rather akin to an incubation period for a bacterial or viral infection, the period in which the poison spreads through the body and begins to wreak its damage. The 'incubation' period is not always of the same duration. Symptoms can appear within half an hour, or may take up to two days to show themselves. The particular danger of the delayed-action poisons is that by the time the major symptoms show, the poison has been well distributed and it is too late to do much about countering its potency.

There are several kinds of poisoning throughout the plant kingdom, by no means limited to fungi, which affect not the stomach but the nervous system. The substances are frequently compounds called alkaloids, complex products of plant metabolism containing nitrogen. The first symptoms may be giddi-ness, increase in saliva and sweat production, heightened perception and general nervous distress.

Irrespective of the kind of poisoning, once symptoms are showing there

[110]

are a number of vital first aid procedures to be followed. The object is essentially twofold: to remove as much of the poison from the patient as is possible, and to slow or stop the spread of that which has penetrated too deeply to be removed by first aid. Then go straight to the nearest casualty unit.

To get rid of any poison in the stomach, the patient must be made to vomit immediately. There are two remarkably effective ways of achieving this on the spur of the moment. Either tickle the uvula at the back of the throat with a feather or a finger (nothing hard like a pencil or a stick). Do not make the patient drink salty water. Salt water treatment can be dangerous, though prescribed in some books.

The person is probably in a state of some panic by now, and it is important to calm them. The slower the pulse rate, the longer the poison will take to spread. Keep the person as still and quiet as possible. If the shock is severe, some sweet tea is a good idea. This will not change the rate at which the poison is absorbed, or make it more difficult to remove later.

The one golden rule is: no alcohol. Contrary to Hollywood dictates, a stiff shot of brandy is not the answer, since it actually works against recovery. Heart and absorption rates are speeded up once alcohol is in the bloodstream.

Thus far, most of the first aid treatment is probably common sense to anyone who has a basic notion of what to do in an emergency. There is one vital job, however, which may be overlooked in the excitement; not a very pleasant task but it may save someone's life. Any uneaten part of the food must be saved for identification, along with a quantity of the material which has been consumed and vomited.

The doctors who will shortly be endeavouring to treat the patient will have very little information to work on. Plant toxins are particularly problematic, because the chemical compounds are complicated by-products of the plant's metabolism, and because the plant also frequently synthesises not one but several different poisonous compounds. So, unless the doctor has an exact understanding of what has been eaten, he may find it extremely difficult to select a suitable treatment.

It is also well worth asking the person for details of where they collected the specimens. More may be growing and can be collected up for proper identification. On this point, however, it is important to bear one other factor in mind.

Irrespective of the personal factor in plant poisoning, the state of the specimen is always important. In all plants, certain chemical changes occur with ageing. Not only do chemicals that were sparse in the young tissues become more concentrated as the plant grows older, but sometimes their nature alters. Poisonous substances may, in other words, turn a harmless young specimen into something less palatable once it has gone beyond its first flush of youth. It is generally accepted that a fungus is past its edible state when you can see worm tunnels in the flesh, though frankly I would prefer to avoid a specimen long before it has reached that state of disrepair.

So, let us get down to specifics. Plant poisoning can be probably measured on a scale of ten, starting at one with the marginal group of otherwise edible fungi which will give the odd susceptible person a tummy ache after eating a plateful. At the other end of the scale are those whose toxins are lethal unless specific therapeutic measures are taken to counter their effects. Between the two extremes there also crop up odd quirks. Certain specimens are described as thermolabile, a scientific term identifying a poisonous substance that is destroyed by heat. Hence a mushroom that is inedible when raw and therefore unsuitable for use in salads, may be perfectly palatable and safe on cooking. But then what is new about that? Red kidney beans have to be cooked to dispel their toxicity, and no one loses any sleep about eating kidney beans!

In medical terms, the toxins produced by various fungi in Britain can be separated into groups. These groups affect the body in different and often fairly distinct ways, and it is important to have some outline knowledge of what is what.

NON-SPECIFIC POISONS

A number of fungi produce poisons which are vague in identity, but which have similar effects on people eating them. Usually the problems begin with severe stomach ache, accompanied by repeated sickness and diarrhoea. This distressing condition can continue for up to a week, and although in itself it is unlikely to prove dangerous to anyone reasonably fit, it can weaken and dehydrate to a point of exhaustion which could be fatal for anyone in poor health, the very young, or the elderly.

It is not unlikely that the specimen mistakenly collected as Agaricus, by Chris and Jane, was in fact *Entoloma sinuatum*, which contains poisons of this type and which looks, at certain stages of development, similar to the common edible mushroom. It grows extensively in southern France and the French, ever with a flair for understatement, call it 'Le Grand Empoisonneur de la Côte d'Or'.

The afore-mentioned Worthington Smith had a brush with this mushroom. He described the taste as being 'by no means disagreeable', but then succumbed to the typical symptoms, believed he was dying fast, and was in fact ill for four or five days before staggering back to the woods for more punishment: '. . . during the latter part of the first day, I was so continually and fearfully purged, and suffered so much from headache and swimming of the brain, that I really thought every moment would be my last. I was very ill for the next four to five days; suffered from loathing and lassitude; fell into deep sleep, long and troubled; at times found all my joints quite stiff; at others everything would be swimming before me; and it was not until a fortnight had elapsed that every bodily derangement had left me.'

E. sinuatum differs from the edible mushroom in that there is no ring on the stem, and the gills start life not pink but yellowish, and then turn salmon pink in the mature cap, whereas those of Agaricus are, by a similar stage of development, chocolate brown.

In the same broad category are the Sickeners (*Russula emetica* and *R. mairei*). The first grows largely under conifers, the latter under beech, but both are similar in appearance. The cap is bright scarlet with white, rather brittle, waxy gills and a white stalk. *R. emetica* is said to have a strongly acrid taste, not shared by *R. mairei*.

Also to be avoided are any of the Boletus family with red pores, and at least one common member of the Agaricus group, the Yellow Stainer (*A. xanthoderma*). It looks remarkably similar to the edible *A. silvicola*, and several of the group stain chrome yellow when bruised or cut. However, only

Russula mairei

A. xanthoderma and a much less frequent form, *A. placomyces*, turn yellow in the extreme base of the stem immediately on cutting. Both also smell distinctively of phenol, or ink, whilst most of the woodland Agaricus members smell of aniseed.

Finally, I should include a curious anomaly, a member of the Amanita group which is sought after in many continental countries and delicious when cooked. The Blusher (*A. rubescens*) is one of those examples of a mushroom that produces thermolabile poisons. Eat it raw and you suffer. Cook it and there are no ill-effects. The Blusher has all the typical characteristics of an Amanita. The cap is a dull reddish brown, covered with small warty clay-coloured patches of the veil. The most obvious clue to the mushroom's identity is a reddening of the flesh when cut, whence the name 'The Blusher'.

Amanita rubescens

ALCOHOL-RELATED POISONS

A couple of the more common Ink Caps (*Coprinus atramentarius* and *C. micaceus*) generate a substance which only takes effect if alcohol is consumed with the mushrooms. In fact the symptoms can appear if alcohol is consumed over several days afterwards. Probably the toxin is largely insoluble in our digestive juices, and therefore harmless until it dissolves in alcohol. It is a complicated chemical, very close in make-up to a man-made compound, tetraethylthiuramdisulphide (a name not to be conjured if you have been drinking).

This has been available for many years, under a well-known brand name, for use in the treatment of chronic alcoholism.

After about twenty minutes the patient flushes dramatically about the face, neck and upper body, whilst the tip of the nose and the ear lobes remain pallid! The heart rate steps up smartly, and the patient experiences considerable discomfort including the sensation of extreme heat. There are no other accountable symptoms, and the effect passes off in an hour or so unless more alcohol is consumed. The toxin is stored in the liver, and is released little by little when there is alcohol in the blood stream.

The Common Ink Cap (*C. atramentarius*) grows in fields and gardens, often pushing up from rotten wood submerged in gravel and tarmac drives. It is usually in dense clumps. The cap is dirty greyish brown and becomes conical to bell-shaped. The gills start life off-white, turning dirty brown and finally black. Like the Shaggy Ink Cap (*C. comatus*), the fruiting body autodigests into a black mush.

The Glistening Ink Cap (*C. micaceus*) also grows tufted on broad-leaf stumps, but it is a smaller, more delicate-looking mushroom, and the caps are covered with tiny whitish mica-like particles.

HELVELLIC ACID POISONING

Coming, in terms of consequences, to the rather more serious forms of fungal toxin, the members of the Helvella group produce an acid which has the effect of breaking down red blood cells in the human body. It is a process technically called haemolysis.

There is something of a dilemma about this kind of poisoning, though, because theoretically helvellic acid is rendered harmless on cooking. However, a related specimen, *Gyromitra esculenta*, which is eaten extensively on the Continent and which also produces helvellic acid, has been the culprit in some rather disturbing anomalies.

Several years ago the curious case of a Canadian family earned extensive news coverage. A mother, father and teenage son collected Gyromitra, soaked them overnight in salted water as they had done on countless occasions in the past, and cooked them for lunch.

Within twelve hours all three were showing the symptoms of fungal poisoning – vomiting, diarrhoea and severe stomach pain. The parents, who had only eaten a little of the fungus, recovered but the son entered a deep coma and died two days later.

Why this tragedy happened, when the family had previously eaten the fungus with apparent immunity, is unclear.

It is thought that there may be more than one active toxin in Gyromitra, and that some part of the complicated poisonous make-up is not destroyed on cooking, but is perhaps accumulated gradually in the liver and kidneys, causing no obvious effect until it reaches a threshold concentration. For this reason I have deliberately avoided inclusion of Gyromitra amongst the edible species.

THE ERGOT POISONS

In the 'good old days', before farmers and growers sprayed nasty agrochemicals all over their crops and modern technology allowed for the effective screening of seed, a strange-looking fungus used to cause a particularly horrific disease amongst people who were obliged to eat their bread made from rye flour. The irony was that for centuries they thought it was all down to divine retribution.

Claviceps purpurea is an Ascomycete, which takes over the 'ears' of certain grasses and cereals. The fruiting body is a black sickle-shaped object, growing to about 2.5 cm in length and called a *sclerotium*. The French coined the name 'ergot' because of the similarity of the growth to a cock's spur. The

Claviceps purpurea

spores of the fungus find their way into the ovary of the grass inflorescence, from whence they develop into a mycelium. In wild grasses the sclerotia fall to the ground in autumn and begin their life cycle over again.

They germinate, in the spring, to tiny fruiting bodies shaped like drumsticks. These in their turn liberate the spores that will infect the current season's grass inflorescences. In cereals, however, prior to the days of fungicides and screening, the sclerotia were inadvertently harvested, unrecognised for the havoc they were destined to cause. They were milled into the flour that provided daily bread for large peasant populations.

Top] *Coprinus atramentarius*   [119]

Bottom] *Helvella crispa*

Thankfully ergotism is largely a thing of the past, though the *Lancet* reported a major outbreak in Ethiopia as recently as 1977, when 136 cases were confirmed in the Wollo region. The last and only major outbreak in Britain, in 1927, caused havoc amongst Jewish immigrants in Manchester.

The people of the British Isles have fared better than the rest of Europe, because historically we have grown wheat in preference to rye for bread-making, and ergot is much less common on wheat. In Europe, though, it has been a different story, and in days gone by, for a victim, the effects were unenviable. The toxins, of which there are now known to be at least a dozen, all based on lysergic acid, have a pronounced effect on the smooth involuntary muscle of the body, causing it to contract. Ergot was popular with midwives in eighteenth centry Europe to speed up delivery because it stimulates the uterus, but in later years ergot was widely abused as a back-street abortifa-cient. Because of its action elsewhere in the body, the side-effects are now considered too dangerous for general medical use, even in controlled dosage.

In mild cases of ergotism, brought on through eating infected bread, the victim used to experience general tiredness with some degree of back pain and aching in the legs. There were often complaints of giddiness, but provided that the ingestion of the fungus did not continue the symptoms disappeared in a week or two.

With habitual consumption of infected bread, however, two distinctly more menacing forms of the disease were waiting. The different forms seem to have been separated geographically, occurring in north eastern and south western Europe, though the reason for this demarcation is still a mystery.

Gangrenous ergotism occurred mainly in France. In its early stages it was characterised by the mild symptoms, but these were soon exacerbated by swelling and inflammation in arms and legs. According to descriptions from victims, they seem to have experienced an alternating sense of extreme heat and cold in the affected parts, accompanied by great pain. The limb then became gradually numbed, the skin bluish and cold to the touch. Dry gangrene was by now inevitable, the limb turning black often with startling suddenness.

If the disease reached this advanced stage, the only satisfactory remedy was amputation. There was a chilling rule of thumb, in medical circles, to rate survival chances. One limb lost probably meant recovery. Two limbs amputated, and the prognosis was fatal. Three, or all four, and the shock was so violent that the victims rarely reached the stage of medical debate. They were dead already.

Gangrenous ergotism has nurtured its stock of bizarre stories. One, on the official medical record, recounts how a woman suffering from advanced gangrene in her leg was riding to hospital on a horse to have the limb removed. A bush by the roadside saved the surgeon's operating expenses. The limb was caught up in the branches and fell off. The lady is said to have continued on her way with the separated leg cradled in her arms. Such was the quality of life in great-grandfather's day.

Convulsive ergotism was equally horrendous, though it seems to have made its presence felt later in history and was mainly confined to Russia and her neighbours. The first recorded outbreak was in 1722, and for fifty years until sorting and cleaning of grain began to take effect, the disease claimed many thousands of lives. Even as late as the 1920s, in some years of poor harvest, ergot poisoning was still reaching epidemic proportions in more remote parts of Russia.

The disease began in a similar manner to that of the gangrenous variety, though often with the sensation of pins and needles: 'ants running about under the skin', as patients frequently described it. The sensation was generally strongest in the fingers and forearms, but could spread to the rest of the body. After a week or so, the more acute symptoms developed with muscular twitching followed by convulsions and paralysis. This was the condition described so graphically in the old woodcuts, attributing the cause of the affliction to St Anthony's Fire – the victim adopting a staggering gait, the limbs and fingers flexed like claws, the mouth wide in a shout of agony.

Ravenous appetite could also accompany the symptoms. Between bouts of convulsion the patient could eat a full meal, yet feel extreme hunger immediately afterwards. There is one record of two victims devouring six pounds of bread between them, in just over five minutes. Deranged victims even ate clothing and faeces to satisfy their craving for food.

Both forms of the disease were fatal, although the convulsive form sometimes took years to kill, with recurrent bouts of madness over a long period of time. Among the more tragic effects was the death in puberty of children that had contracted the disease many years earlier and apparently made a full recovery.

MUSCARINE AND MYCOATROPINE POISONING

The best known species producing the toxin muscarine is, of course, the Fly Agaric (*Amanita muscaria*). Muscarine is also produced by a number of other fairly common mushrooms including the two small Clitocybes which often occur with Fairy Ring Champignon, *C. rivulosa* and *C. dealbeata*, and by a number of the Inocybe group, none of which frankly look palatable enough to eat! A photograph of *C. dealbeata* is shown, and at first glance *C. rivulosa* looks very similar. Both are off-white, against the buff of the edible Champignon, and their gills are much closer together.

It is another of the alkaloid toxins, but it has been calculated that you would have to eat at least 250 grams of fresh poisonous specimens to take in a lethal dose, and even in the Inocybe group which contain the highest concentrations, any smaller intake would be unlikely to kill a healthy individual.

Muscarine symptoms include production of a great deal of sweat and tears, as well as copious secretions from the mucous membranes of nose and throat. Also in the list of effects are sickness, diarrhoea and stomach cramps. Asthmatic breathing, double vision, loss of blood pressure and a sensation of cold in hands and feet are also typical of muscarine poisoning. In mild cases the symptoms disappear fairly rapidly, but if enough of the poison has been ingested coma and death from respiratory failure ensue.

Mycoatropine is found in two of the Amanitas, Fly Agaric (*A. muscaria*) and Panther Cap (*A. pantherina*). Like muscarine, it works on the central nervous system with symptoms appearing from half an hour to four hours after eating the mushroom. The senses become heightened, the patient may experience giddiness and possibly go into a trance. Consuming mycoatropine is unlikely to be fatal, though, unless the victim has been in a particularly poor state of health.

[122]   *Top*] *Clitocybe dealbeata*

Bottom] *Amanita muscaria*

THE AMANITA POISONS

We are now into decidedly unpleasant and fatal realms, though occasional recoveries from these toxins have been known. Taken as a whole, the chemicals in this category represent some of the most dangerous substances known to medical science. Their effect on the human body is violent and extreme.

The most lethal of the Amanitas are the Death Cap (*A. phalloides*); the Destroying Angel (*A. virosa*); the extremely rare Spring Amanita (*A. verna*); and the equally infrequent autumn species *A. gemmata*. All four are deadly poisonous even in very small quantities, and unfortunately neither Death Cap nor Destroying Angel bear the tell-tale velar patches on the cap that characterise most other Amanitas.

The Death Cap (*A. phalloides*) has a large, convex then flattened, characteristically greenish olive cap streaked with faint radiating fibres. The gills and stem are pure white. There is an obvious floppy, pendulous ring and a large volval bag above the basal bulb. There also occurs in some years a pure white variety of *A. phalloides*.

The Destroying Angel(*A. virosa*), an apt title, is a pure innocent white. It tends to grow taller and more imposing than Death Cap, with a cap that is at first conical to bell-shaped but also devoid of patches and with a somewhat shaggy stem.

Both species appear in the autumn in mixed or deciduous woods, and Death Cap is often found in close association with oaks.

These fungi produce two kinds of organic compounds known as crystalline cyclo-peptides. One group, called phallotoxins, is destroyed by heat and therefore rendered innocuous by cooking. None of these should be eaten raw.

They include the substances phalloidin, phalloin, phallicidin, phallisin and phallin B some of which, apart from being thermolabile, are also knocked out by digestive juices. Phallin B has an intensely destructive effect on red blood cells, even when present in very minute quantities (one part in 125,000).

Amanita poisoning is characterised by extensive destruction of tissues in the body, the attack being made irrespective of cooking. The responsibility for this damage lies with the second group of poisons, the alpha and beta amanita toxins, amongst which at least six separate substances are known. One of the traits which makes them so dangerous is that they are comparatively slow-acting. There is often a delay of more than twelve hours before the first symptoms of poisoning appear, by which time the toxins have spread throughout the body. They attack the nuclei of human cells which then start, irreversibly, to break up.

The symptoms begin with a period of intensive vomiting and diarrhoea, which may appear as little more than a virulent stomach upset. Towards the end of the first day, the skin may turn pallid or bluish; sometimes there is an appearance of jaundice, and the victim may undergo convulsions. One of the unusual aspects of the poisoning is that there are frequently periods of remission, during which the patient seems almost recovered. During the second day, though, circulatory failure begins to take more serious effect, the pulse becomes very weak and there is almost total loss of recordable blood pressure.

At this point in the course of poisoning, chances of recovery depend on precisely how much damage has been sustained by vital organs, particularly the liver, kidneys and heart.

Another curious anomaly of Amanita poisoning is that herbivores like rabbits seem totally immune to its effect, whilst dogs and cats suffer in a similar way to humans. Because of the rabbit's immunity, there was for a long time a bizarre treatment, widely practised in France, which involved feeding the patient with the brains and stomachs of rabbits.

Then in the autumn of 1973, a dramatic case of Amanita poisoning led to the adoption of a slightly less dark-age method of treatment. In Guernsey, Michael and Linda le Coq innocently collected, cooked and ate about half a dozen specimens of Death Cap. On the following morning, a local doctor was called to treat what he believed was a case of common food poisoning. After another 48 hours, however, the couple were extremely weak and clearly very ill.

Michael was in an advanced state of shock, and both he and Linda were moved to hospital. The attending physician at this stage managed to obtain some more of the mushrooms, and correctly identified them.

From that moment, the treatment to save the Le Coqs moved into a new gear, and as part of routine procedure, first the Poisons Centre at Guy's Hospital in London, and then the Intensive Care Liver Unit at King's College Hospital were notified. The now critically ill patients were flown to London. Linda le Coq was giving particular cause for concern, because she was known to be suffering from acute liver damage. Michael, who had suffered more violently in the early stages, slowly began to recover. Linda lapsed into a coma.

The leader of the medical team resorted to an almost untried technique, filtering the patient's blood through a carbon column dialysis machine. Linda made medical history. No other victim with that amount of tissue damage had survived before, but the treatment worked and Linda left hospital to begin her recuperation three long weeks after eating her deadly breakfast.

You may wonder why I include these details in what is otherwise intended to be a light-hearted, celebratory book. Well, part of the fear of fungi lies in lack of knowledge, the unknown horrors of their powers. I am trying to put the record straight, to balance the good against the bad. Let us finish this rather depressing side of things by putting the whole question of fungal poisons back into perspective.

There is a short film, a cameo gem which most people must have seen at one time or another, a driver's-eye-view of the train journey between London and Brighton speeded up to just four minutes duration.

A fair analogy can be made, even if you have never stepped aboard the Brighton Belle at Victoria Station. If all the 3500 or so species of larger mushrooms and toadstools found in Britain were laid evenly spaced along the track, those which are good edible specimens would fit neatly under the long canopy of Victoria. All through the London suburbs and the countryside down to the coast, the track would be lined by the vast bulk of specimens, inoffensive but uninteresting to the gourmet. Along the much smaller platform at Brighton, there would be more than enough space to fit the tiny fraction of 'nasties'. Bear in mind also, that of those few specimens, only those producing muscarine and amanita compounds are deadly dangerous for most

Amanita phalloides

people. That is the true picture.

Some of the poisonous members turn up quite regularly in the season, but then so do privet and buttercup, yew and buckthorn, and you would not think of eating those! The statistics speak for themselves. In the whole of the United Kingdom during the last twenty years, there have been just seven fatalities from eating poisonous fungi, most of those attributable to the Death Cap.

[127]

A small but bizarre post-script to the subject of fungal poisoning appeared in the *Independent* newspaper on August 29th, 1988. In that season radio-activity levels in Norwegian sheep, monitored since the 1986 Chernobyl nuclear disaster, were found to be abnormally high again and the culprits were identified as fungi. A bumper crop appeared in Scandinavia, which were in turn eaten by the sheep.

Fungi are known to accumulate radio-active isotopes of the element caesium, which was released in huge quantities by the Chernobyl explosion, and of which about a kilogramme is thought to have fallen on Norway. Twelve thousand contaminated sheep had to be 'flushed' on a caesium-free diet after their gorge on the radio-active plants.

When all things are considered, our fear and even loathing of all those fungi with which we are not absolutely familiar, and which we tend automatically to label as toadstools, is quite illogical. Curiously, the Death Cap (*A. phalloides*) has featured very little in our history. It has only affected those limited numbers who have fallen victim to its effects.

If there is one species which has spiced our horror about these marvellous plants, it has to be the Fly Agaric (*A. muscaria*). It was this remarkable growth about which all the early taboos were raised. Alas, even dear old Noddy has not quite been able to break the mould.

8
Lore and Legend

1989 marks Noddy's fortieth birthday! If ever there was a Grand Prix to be awarded to someone who has popularised fungal mythology in modern times, it should surely go to Enid Blyton with her familiar red and white spotted toadstools. It is a shame that they happen to be dangerously poisonous, but we cannot have everything and neither Noddy nor Big Ears seems to have suffered from proximity to *Amanita muscaria* during the better part of half a century.

Fungi have enjoyed a fairly sensational ride down the pages of folklore. The ageless intrigue attached to them is not altogether surprising when you consider what they are and how they grow. Their shape is like nothing else in nature, though in the young state many mushrooms appear distinctly phallic with all that that implies. In fact many of the early physicians and herbalists were undecided whether fungi should be regarded as plants, or animals, or some distinctly separate life form.

They grow with the most garish colours, again often quite foreign to the rest of the green world. They also appear with astonishing speed after rain, a cause for speculation since to most primitive people rain is a fertilising power from the heavens, the product of some mighty celestial ejaculation.

Perhaps most significantly of all, they have the powers to unlock the secrets of the mystical world.

The hallucinogenic drugs produced by some fungi, not least among them the Fly Agaric (*A. muscaria*), are seen as the doorway to the spirit plane.

The nomadic hunting tribes of northern Europe and Asia were familiar with Fly Agaric. A Swedish-American ethnologist, Waldemar Jochelson, visited some remote tribes in eastern Siberia at the turn of the century and brought back reports of their reliance on Fly Agaric for inducing shamanistic trances. One such tribe, the Koryak, believed that spirits known as the Wapag Men inhabited the fungus which grew around the wooded shores of the Sea of Okhotsk on the Kamchatka archipelago. The spirits of the woods had chosen to leave these fungi for the benefit of mankind to reveal what lay beyond the temporal world. Predictably many stories grew up amongst the Koryak and other tribes on the subject of the Wapag and their remarkable powers.

Jochelson brought back one slightly bizarre account of a group of elderly shamans sharing out a quantity of Fly Agaric, the source for which was in particularly short supply. The most senior shaman chewed on the available dried caps, entered his trance and then urinated into a tin can. The next most senior in the group promptly drank the contents and continued the process on to the next man. The object of this unlikely exercise, pass the parcel with a difference, relies on the fact that the muscarine and mycoatropine are passed rapidly through the blood stream and into the kidneys!

Certainly most tribal societies from the Arctic to the Equator rely on one sort of hallucinogenic mushroom or another, as part of their culture. In Scandinavia, the equivalent of modern-day lager louts, known as the Berserks, used regularly to get high on Fly Agaric and terrorise the countryside in large marauding gangs.

If there is twentieth century mythology about fungi, it lies principally with the slim, innocuous-looking Liberty Cap (*Psilocybe semi-lanceolata*). The information is, of course, strictly unofficial, but eminent persons have been known to trek stealthily through the wilds of Hampstead Heath on a misty autumn morning on the lookout for slim little caps poking through the dewy grass. Stockbrokers and students, bank managers and bus conductors will at times coyly produce an envelope of 'magic mushroom' and sums of money will change hands. A clandestine Psilocybe festival is actually held each year at a discreet location in the depths of Wales.

Our 'supplier' was located in Gloucestershire and lured over the border to show us the whereabouts of some nice specimens. Thankfully blindfolds were not insisted upon, but you will understand that I am sworn to reticence on the map reference!

A number of small grassland fungi which are not uncommon in Britain produce the chemicals psilocin and psilocybin. Until 1958, when these active ingredients were isolated by Dr Albert Hoffman of LSD fame, their identity, though not their effects, was virtually unknown.

Effects-wise, the properties of these hallucinogenic fungi were probably familiar to most witches in pre-industrial times, and their descent into comparative obscurity no doubt began with the persecution of witches in the Middle Ages.

In many parts of Central and South America, the 'magic mushroom' is of enormous social value and implication. *Psilocybe mexicana* is frequently employed by elderly women dispensing their magic and cures in the villages. It is closely related to our own locally grown Liberty Cap.

Other mushrooms which generate the drugs include several Panaeolus, Stropharia and Hypholoma species. The effects of a moderate dose of the fresh or dried material are said to include heightened perception, both visual and auditory, and a feeling of euphoria. The symptoms commence after about twenty minutes and can continue for eight or nine hours, the hallucinations becoming stronger as time passes. Milder effects can then continue on and off for several days and even weeks.

It seems that you do not have to go such lengths to blow your mind, incidentally. If you are a muesli-person, you may, according to newspaper reports, be getting your kicks at breakfast time. Dr David Conning, Director-General of the British Nutrition Foundation, believes, the reports say, that small amounts of ergot may still be finding their way into cereals, and ergot produces, among its arsenal of toxins, LSD. Predictably, the manufacturers of breakfast cereals are not impressed by Dr Conning.

Fungi seem to have produced their fair share of notorious substances. Some of the most bizarre folklore surrounds the Ergot Fungus (*Claviceps purpurea*). During the first half of the eleventh centry, Europe experienced horrific epidemics of ergotism, though nobody seems to have connected the disease with the fungal sclerotia growing on the rye used as the staple source of bread. By the twelfth centry, the disease was being linked to St Anthony.

St Anthony was a remarkable hermit who lived in Egypt in the third century A.D., and who was believed to have powers over fire. Many of the old illustrations of the disease picture victims holding out arms to St Anthony, from which flames are pouring. The disease came to be known by several names with clear religious connotations. In France it was 'Le Feu de St Antoine', and 'Ignis Sacer', the sacred fire. It was also given the title 'Ignis Beatae Virginis', the fire of the Blessed Virgin.

Ironically, the small black ergots infesting the rye fields of medieval Europe were regarded as evidence of the passing of the Corn Mother, who was a beneficial goddess. Meanwhile, after the bones of St Anthony were interred at their final resting place in the Church of La Motte au Bois in Vienne, local stories of miraculous cures for the disease now recognised as ergotism began to spread. A hospital was built specifically catering for victims of the Sacred Fire.

It was not until 1771, though, that the French Abbé Teissier made positive links between ergot sclerotia and the disease. He experimented, using pigs and ducks for his tests, and discovered that they developed the characteristic symptoms after being fed with infected rye.

It is a provocative thought, that if the 'greenhouse effect' is indeed taking effect, and our summers are going to be warmer and wetter, such fungi will be all the more difficult to keep at bay.

Mythology has generated some bizarre notions about fungi. The Greek writer Theophrastus, who lived in the fourth century B.C., wrote a discourse on plants in which he comments:

In the sea around the Pillars of Hercules where there is much water, fungi are produced close to the sea, which people say have been turned to stone by the sun.

The objects he was describing were in fact 'stone corals'. Their generally mushroom-like appearance with radiating plates of calcareous material added to the deception and people really believed that they were seeing petrified mushrooms.

Some fungi possess the property of luminescence, virtually guaranteed to get the minds of the less technologically conversant agog with speculation.

St Anthony and a victim of his fire,
reproduced in Ergot and Ergotism *by G. Barger (1931)*

The eighth century *Beowulf* saga includes this reference to them:

It is not far from here if measured in miles, that the lake stands shadowed by trees stiff with hoar frost. A wood, firmly rooted, frowns over the water.
There, night after night, a fearful wonder may be seen – fire on the water ... that is not a pleasant place.

One of the most common mushrooms growing on rotten stumps, the Honey Fungus (*Armillarea mellea*), produces luminescence and it or some species like it was inevitably at the root of the 'fire on the water'. It is not actually the fruiting body, but the actively growing tips of the mycelia which produce the effect. Hence, the thick 'bootlace' rhizomorphs cause the wood to glow.

Luminous wood has been well-known for centuries to people living in or near forests. There are frequent references to it in literature. Even Mark Twain in his *Adventures of Huckleberry Finn* includes a comment about 'foxfire' emanating from chunks of rotten wood that make a soft kind of glow when laid in a dark place.

Curious notions about luminous wood were slow to die. They were still rife as late as the Second World War. London timber yards were found to be glowing at night, offering a potential beacon for enemy aircraft. They were thought to have been dusted with phosphorus from German incendiary bombs. The problem was in fact down to the Honey Fungus 'home guard'.

More than any other single mycological phenomenon, it is perhaps the 'Fairy Ring' which is associated with fungal lore and legend in most people's minds. It is the age-old haunt of dancing witches, and the 'little people'. Shakespeare's *The Tempest* includes this comment by Prospero:

You demi-puppets that
By moonshine do the green sour ringlets make,
whereof ewe not bites; and you, whose pastime
is to make midnight mushrumps ...

The early herbalists had no idea of the cause of these strange emanations, so the suggestions which they put forward in explanation were frequently rather eccentric. Clearly the rings were believed to be places of magic and supernatural powers. One of the most common explanations in folklore has been that either fairies or witches, depending upon the authority to which you subscribe, danced round within the circles doing unspeakable things at such times as May Day eve, and the mushrooms were left behind as a mark of their presence. In Austria, there was a variation on the theme, with a winged dragon flying round and round in circles, scorching the grass with his breath.

The deadened appearance of the grass within the circle, an after-effect of the stimulation caused by the actively growing mycelium, prompted several myths about scorching. More scientifically-minded people, presumably with a leaning towards physics, put the phenomenon down to lightning.

Some of the scientific explanations came perilously close to the lunatic themselves. The widely respected eighteenth century observer Bradley made the astute observation that fairy rings were associated with the appearance of mushrooms. It was his opinion, however, that the sex-lives of slugs and snails were at the heart of the matter. He had watched them perambulating in amorous circles on the lawn, going round and round several times before getting down to the serious business of producing little molluscs. With each circuit, they left a trail of slime which, according to Bradley, putrefied and so gave rise to the mushrooms.

Bradley was in fact paying lip-service to a very old belief, going back to Greek and Roman times, that fungi were the 'crystallisation' of poisonous or otherwise noxious substances, generated in bogs and left by other creatures of a generally poisonous disposition.

Other explanations on the more biological theme attributed fairy rings to the work of moles conducting their mining operations in circles, and to the possibility that cattle standing in a circle, heads inwards and munching on their hay feed, would of necessity leave their cow pats in a neat circular arrangement!

It was actually one of the more eloquent mycologists of the eighteenth century, William Withering, who put the matter straight scientifically and linked the rings to the growth of *Marasmius oreades*.

According to Philip Findlay, a one-time president of the British Mycological Society, there exists an old superstition about the cosmetic disadvantages of the fairy ring. It was said that if a young girl went to bathe her face in the early dew of a May morn, her comeliness would increase. If, however, by accident she performed her toilette within the circle of a fairy ring, the fairies would take umbrage, and her skin would erupt in blemishes and spots. I have not tested the theory personally, but would probably recommend my daughter to steer clear of experimenting.

On the other hand, as is so often the case with folklore, there was an antithesis and some people believed it lucky to have a fairy ring in the garden.

So why is it that some nationalities are so much in love with mushrooms and toadstools, yet others possess a virulent loathing? I suspect that in the long run, if you trace back far enough it is largely down to the extent to which our forebears were subject to influence by the Greeks and Romans. Today, you will find the champions of things mycological by and large living around the Mediterranean, though also in much of central Europe.

In such regions the language of the mushroom and its virtues is universal from childhood. Mushrooms of all shades are friends, and accidents are few. You have to follow the paths of Germanic and Celtic influence to find the other side of the coin, and these were peoples who, historically, were deprived of the good offices of the great classical empire builders.

I nurse the hope that the Channel 4 television series and this slim volume will do something to redress the balance. Fungi have given me much pleasure over the years; wandering the gentle autumn woodlands rich with the smells of old bracken and damp earth; finding a personal store of new and undiscovered species; carrying home prizes and cooking them amidst the shock and disbelief of friends and family; just revelling in the delight of some of the most astonishing forms of life on God's earth.

Appendices

APPENDIX 1

A Guide to the Major Genera

If you are making a start on fungus hunting, there are several categories which should not present too many headaches, and which incidentally contain most of the 'nice and nasty' jobs. This appendix is not intended to be a thorough 'key', but a gentle ramble through the larger groups which you are most likely to encounter when you make your first trip to the woods in search of fungi.

It is based on the biological classification of the two groups of Higher Fungi, Basidiomycetes and Ascomycetes.

Basidiomycetes

are separated into four chief sections:

1 APHYLLOPHORALES
a] *Bracket Fungi*
These are included in the group known as 'Polypores' (*Polyporaceae*). They grow on wood. Some, like the Birch Bracket (*Piptoporus betulinus*) are parasites which cause extensive damage to living timber. Birch Bracket is one of the chief attackers of birch trees, causing decay and finally death of the sapwood. Many live off dead and dying wood. One of the commonest is *Coriolus versicolor* which sprouts in dense tiers on felled timber, and will in time completely rot the wood.

The brackets present an ideal teething ground for beginners. There are not too many of them growing in the British Isles. Most are quite distinctive in appearance, and many are restricted to one particular kind of host timber. They tend also to be present throughout much of the year, so you do not have to wait until autumn to get to grips with them. Beware of appearances though. Owing to the fact that many of them retain durable shape, even when dead, they are not always as described in the field guide. A specimen called *Inonotus hispidus*, which is quite common on old ash trees, appears as a brownish bracket in autumn but dies off to look like a sooty 'rarity' that can persist through much of the year.

The brackets are linked in the common possession of tubes, opening by pores through which their spores are liberated, hence the name Polypores. In the more advanced forms, the tubes open on the underneath of the bracket, but in some of the simple resupinate families, including *Peniophora*, the fertile layer is on top. There is

[139]

an intermediate stage to be seen in the *Stereum* family, where the fruiting body is slightly thicker and forms a partly encrusting, partly projecting bracket, with the fertile layer on the undersurface.

In their most elaborate, and incidentally most dramatic form, the brackets appear as tough, corky growths which are often substantial and survive throughout the year. Sometimes they appear singly, like the Birch Bracket, or they build up in massive tiers on the tree trunk.

Ganoderma applanatum, the so-called Artists' Fungus, can develop into a mighty structure, with layer upon layer of brackets, each measuring up to 60cm across.

Some are no less startling in appearance, but are softer, annual growths emerging in late summer and dying back with the first heavy frosts. These include the Poor Man's Beefsteak (*Fistulina hepatica*) which although it causes rot in hardwoods like oak, also discolours the timber a tastefully rich brown and so, ironically, is much in demand from furniture makers!

One that is worth keeping an eye open for, is the Chicken of the Woods (*Laetiporus sulphureus*) which takes on a startling lumpy, lemon yellow appearance.

In their simpler forms the brackets are quite small and delicate and ultimately, in types like Peniophora, appear as flat crusts plastered on to the surface of the wood. The most notorious member of the group is one which you won't find in the woods, the Dry Rot Fungus (*Serpula lacrymans*).

The same overall group of fungi to which the Polypores belong, also includes one or two other easily recognisable groups.

b] *Fairy Clubs*

The simplest are the *Clavaria* and *Ramaria* families. All grow upright with club shaped fruiting bodies which are either simple or branched, and which in the Ramarias tend to be densely tufted like corals.

The spore-bearing surface covers the upper ends of the clubs. They are comparatively small species and most grow on soil though a few, including one of the commonest, *Ramaria stricta*, are on buried wood.

One very distinctive fungus which always causes near hysterical excitement when anyone finds it on a fungus hunt, and which is a close relation of the fairy clubs, is the Cauliflower Fungus (*Sparassis crispa*). It is not uncommon, growing right at the base of conifer trees. Sparassis can be quite large, is impossible to confuse with anything else, and is definitely one of the more dramatic finds!

c] *Tooth and Horn Fungi*

Another small related group, is made up of the Tooth or Hedgehog fungi. They look like a typical mushroom with a cap on a stalk, until you turn them over. Then the difference is obvious because instead of gills or pores they sprout masses of tiny downwardly-projecting teeth from which the spores are shed.

Equally easy to identify and remember, are the Craterellus and Cantharellus 'Horn Fungi'. These include the Horn of Plenty (*Craterellus cornucopoides*) and the famous Chanterelle (*Cantharellus cibarius*). All are funnel-shaped when they mature, and instead of gills they develop blunt branched and rather wrinkly ridges.

2 AGARICALES
Gill Fungi

These are commonly referred to as the 'Agarics'. The group includes all the specimens which most people would regard as mushrooms and toadstools, and there are an awful lot of them! The Agaricales are 'keyed', in most reference books, into groups according to the colour of their spores:

a] *spores which are white, less frequently pale pink or cream, but also red, blue or lilac.*

AMANITA The most dangerous family, including the 'Death Caps'. It is worth getting to know the appearance of each one. There are only about half a dozen which you are likely to come across with any frequency. Most have distinct white patches on their caps, the remains of the veil which protected them as 'buttons'. Unlike scales, these patches or warts are detachable. The gills are always pure white. There is usually a ring on the stem, and at the bulbous base there is typically the remains of a second veil which persists either as a bag, the volva, or as a distinct ridge.

LEPIOTA A group including the large 'Parasols'. Generally easy to spot although there are small members of the group which require more thorough knowledge. All have scaly caps, and all the common members have white gills. Stems bear rings and a useful tip is to try and 'screw' the cap off the stem. In Lepiotas the cap detaches easily. Many have a bulbous base. The group includes both poisonous and edible members, though all the poisonous species are small and none are generally regarded as dangerous.

These two groups, Amanita and Lepiota, share certain common features but also have individual combinations which allow them to be easily distinguished.

LACTARIUS The Milk Caps are perhaps the easiest family of Agarics to recognise because amongst the larger fleshy fungi they are unique in the production of a milky juice, which oozes out of the tissue when damaged. After a few trips to the woods, experience will enable you instinctively to put a group name to many fungi, merely by the general look of them. Lactarius on the whole look like Lactarius, though if you ask me to pinpoint why, I can't! (It is like trying to explain why a poppy looks the way it does.) The certainty comes by gently breaking apart a few of the gills. After a few moments the milk exudes, and you can say with total and impressive confidence that you are holding a Lactarius. Working out which Lactarius may take a little longer. As with any of the other groups, concentrate on getting to grips with one or two of the easier and more common species first.

L. deliciosus is very distinctive and produces carrot-coloured juice; *L. camphoratus* is easy to recognise if you use your nose because it reeks of curry; *L. vellereus* is large white and velvety with the gills well separated.

RUSSULA A large and very prolific group which is worth getting to know early on. The cap in these medium-to-large fungi is often brightly coloured, and the gills range from white to yellow.

Unlike the Lactarius group they produce no milk when damaged, and the stalk is characteristically brittle. It snaps easily. Russulas have neither a ring nor a bulbous tip to the stem. Look out for some of the really common ones, like the yellow *R. ochroleuca*, and the pillar box red *R. emetica* and *R. mairei*. Smell is very important with Russulas. *R. xerampelina* smells of old fish, *R. fellea* of geraniums.

TRICHOLOMA A large rambling family which are less easy to spot. Apart from the fact that they have sinuate gills, no one has yet been able to offer me a sure-fire way of recognising a Tricholoma. Two which used to be included in the family but are now regarded as close cousins in their own separate family, *Lepista nuda* and *L. saeva*, are the 'blewits' and these need to be identified because they are some of the very best for the table. Otherwise the message is, take the group gently and don't lose any sleep over sorting them out. If you are trying to identify Tricholoma, look for one or two of the common ones which also have strong identifying features.

Plums and Custard (*Tricholomopsis rutilans*) is very frequent and distinctive on old conifer stumps, and in most years the bright sulphur yellow *Tricholoma sulphureum* is easy to spot because of its colour.

CLITOCYBE A largish and important family of Agarics. There are 58 members in the British Isles. All bear white gills which are decurrent, sometimes very strongly so, running down the stem. The caps tend to be funnel-shaped and the members often smell of aniseed or have a slightly mealy aroma.

The Clouded Agaric (*C. nebularis*) is one that you are most likely to come across, often in quite large troops. Look out, too, for a smaller specimen, the Aniseed Agaric (*C. odora*), not only a very pretty bluish-green colour but smelling and tasting strongly of aniseed.

COLLYBIA A smallish family of 35 British species, including some very common members like Spotted Tough Shank (*C. maculata*) and Wood Woolly Foot (*C. peronata*). Distinguished by tough fibrous stems, rather crowded gills and the absence of a ring or volva.

MYCENA and MARASMIUS A duo which includes many of the smaller, more delicate woodland species.

The Mycenas are small, sometimes minute fungi with white or greyish gills, and long slender stems often with a polished look to them. Some ooze a juice when the stem is broken. There are more than a hundred species in Britain, and the guide books tend to list only a dozen or so of the commoner types. Look out particularly for three common members with highly distinctive features. *M. galopus* is small, greyish and oozes white latex when the stem is snapped. *M. alcalina* is larger, also a dull grey, and smells very strongly of nitric acid. *M. pura* has a delicate rose pink or lilac tint and smells of radishes when bruised.

Marasmius are also tiny by and large, but are remarkably tough and have considerable powers of rejuvenation after periods of drought when they tend to go very shrivelled and lifeless. They include the famed Fairy Ring Mushroom (*M. oreades*) and the tiny, delightful Horsehair Fungus (*M. androsaceus*) which often carpets pine forest in late autumn. Keep an eye out also for pretty little festoons of white *M. ramealis* on dead twigs.

In general, the caps of Mycena are bell-shaped or conical, whilst those of Marasmius are flatter.

b] *spores which are deep salmon pink. Gills white at first then spore-coloured.*

PLUTEUS A comparatively small family most members of which grow on wood. *P. cervinus* is the commonest on rotting deciduous stumps.

RHODOPHYLLUS, ENTOLOMA, NOLANEA Three families of smallish fungi growing mostly on soil, and all characterised by the development of pink spores. Worth recognising *E. sinuatum* because of its poisonous nature but otherwise these groups are probably better left for a while.

c] *spores which are rusty or clay coloured.*

HEBELOMA Medium fleshy species on soil with smooth, sometimes greasy caps, and clay coloured gills. Look out for Poison Pie (*H. crustuliniforme*), very common and with distinctive white flecking at the top of the stem.

PAXILLUS This is a one-off, as far as common members are concerned. *P. involutus* has strongly decurrent dull brown gills and a slightly shaggy inrolled cap margin.

CORTINARIUS An enormous family which includes an alarming number of 'little brown jobs'. Strictly for the advanced student! The Cortinarius family is dauntingly spread, and certain dedicated mycophiles spend their entire lives interested in very little other than these species. All produce rusty brown coloured spores which shade the gills, and when young each fruiting body is protected by a cobwebby veil, bits of which may remain for some time either attached to the cap or as a fragile ring on the stem.

Other than with a few very distinctive members, someone beginning to delve into fungus identification will earn more headaches than joy with Cortinarius species.

d] *spores which are chocolate brown or black.*

AGARICUS The mushrooms we all know, including the specimen that turns up in the greengrocer's.

Unfortunately, the family shares certain characteristics with the dangerous Amanitas. The similarities have been responsible for most of the reported deaths from eating wild mushrooms.

It is very unfortunate because by following a few simple rules of observation the mistakes can be confidently avoided. The caps are either smooth and whitish, or have scales with one end attached and one end free. This distinguishes them from the patches on an Amanita cap. Gills may be white at first, but very soon become pink and then brown.

There is a ring on the stem, as in the Amanitas, but whilst the base of the stem may be bulbous it never has a ring or ridge round its upper margin.

HYPHOLOMA Several common members and including the Agaric which can probably claim to be commonest of all, Sulphur Tuft (*H. fasciculare*). Very easy to spot with sulphur yellow caps and gills becoming olive green then chocolate. On deciduous stumps.

PSATHYRELLA. PANAEOLUS. STROPHARIA Smallish species mainly in grass and including many of the hallucinogenics. Not easy to identify without experience.

There are other smaller families of agarics, some of which include well known members. It would be confusing to include them in a book of this kind, but it is surprising how quickly the eye comes to recognise many at a glance.

2 AGARICALES
Pore Fungi

Another group of large fleshy 'mushrooms' which are instantly recognisable because all possess pores instead of gills. The most significant features of this quite extensive family lie in the combinations of cap and pore colour.

Equally important are any changes in colour when the flesh is bruised or cut. There are, for instance, several with rather dingy brown caps but only one of them cracks or scrapes to show coral red flesh underneath, *Boletus chrysenteron*.

Nowadays this group is divided into several sub-families: Boletus, Suillus, and Leccinium are the most important.

3 GASTEROMYCETALES
Puff Balls and Earth Balls
Unlike any of the fungi looked at so far, these develop their spores inside the fruiting body, which is more or less rounded. Once ripe, the coat of the sporophore splits or decomposes and the spores are freed. Most grow on soil though at least one species is found on wood. They are related to earth stars (*Geastrum*) and to Bird's Nest Fungi (*Cyathus* and *Crucibulum*), and to the extraordinary Stinkhorns (*Phallus* and *Mutinus*) in which the spore mass rears up over night from an 'egg', and is surmounted on the end of a spongy stalk, embedded in a smelly slime.

4 TREMELLALES
Jelly Fungi
This is a small and unique group of oddly shaped fungi which are rubbery or gelatinous when wet but have great powers of withstanding drought. They include, among others, the extraordinarily beautiful Jelly Hedgehog (*Pseudohydnum gelatinosum*) and the equally bizarre Jew's Ear (*Auricularia auricula*), as well as the pretty, and very common Stag's Horn (*Calocera viscosa*). There are so few of them that they become familiar quickly.

Ascomycetes
The species which you will encounter in the woods and fields
are much less numerous than Basidiomycetes,
though they fall less easily into readily identifiable groups.

1 PEZIZALES
Cup Fungi
These species grow on soil, very often on burnt ground, and a number of them appear in spring. *Peziza badia* is probably the commonest, but also look out for Orange Peel Fungus (*Aleuria aurantia*). The fertile hymenium is spread over the upper surface of the saucer-shaped fruiting body and there is no obvious stem.

2 HELVELLA and MORCHELLA

In helvellas and morels the fertile layer is raised up on to a stalk. The helvellas produce mostly folded saddle-shaped heads.

Morels bear cone-shaped caps pitted into a honeycomb appearance. Note in the guide book those that are vernal (appearing in spring). Some helvellas are vernal, others are autumnal. Morels are all vernal species.

3 TUBERALES
Truffles

Tuberous underground fruiting bodies, difficult to find. *Tuber aestivum*, the British Summer Truffle, is probably the commonest, under beeches and evergreen oaks in the south of England.

4 OTHER GROUPS

There is, finally, a loose assortment of larger Ascomycetes, including Ergot (*Claviceps*); Earth Tongues (*Geoglossum*); various spherical fruiting bodies including common forms like *Helotium citrinum*; irregular discs including *Bulgaria inquinans* and *Coryne sarcoides*; club-shaped sporophores including Candle Snuff Fungus (*Xylaria hypoxylon*) and Dead Man's Fingers (*X. polymorpha*).

There is no simple rule-of-thumb way to recognise these assorted species, but all have such individual appearance that they are learned easily.

HALLUCINOGENS

Certain specimens have been included in both this book and the television series which contains hallucinogenic chemicals.

These substances are dangerous. The organisation RELEASE which aims to advise and help those who experiment with such substances says:

"Eating mushrooms reputed to have hallucinogenic properties has recently become popular. Release is concerned because many people seem totally ignorant of the dangers involved."

RELEASE produces a pamphlet outlining the risks and giving positive advice. It can be obtained from:

RELEASE, 169 Commercial Street, London E1. (telephone 01–603–8654)

APPENDIX 2

Mushroom Recipes

BACON AND OYSTERCAP ROLLS [makes 8]

60gm (2oz) chopped oystercaps
60gm (2oz) fresh breadcrumbs
3 small shallots, finely chopped
225gm (8oz) back bacon
1 egg
Mixed herbs
Seasoning

Mix the fresh breadcrumbs, chopped shallots and mushrooms together, adding herbs and seasoning to taste; beat the egg and stir into the mixture. Spread the mixture evenly on the bacon rashers. Roll and secure with a cocktail stick. Grill for 10 minutes, turning once, or bake in a moderate oven at 160°C (Gas Mark 3) for 20 minutes. Serve either as a party snack, or on a bed of macaroni cheese.

BLEWIT VEGETARIAN CASSEROLE [serves 4]

335gm (12oz) Blewit mushrooms, diced
4 courgettes, sliced
2 onions, chopped
225gm (8oz) dry pasta shells
2 bananas, sliced
390gm (14oz) pineapple, diced
1tbsp cornflour
110gm (4oz) margarine or cooking oil
1 clove garlic
Cupful red wine
15ml (1tbsp) soya sauce
Seasoning

Soften the chopped onion in margarine or oil, add the courgettes and Blewits and cook gently for 5 minutes. Cook the pasta shells in boiling salted water for 5–10 minutes and drain. Add Blewit mixture with pineapple and banana, stirring well. Blend the cornflour with the red wine, soya sauce and a little water (or juice from canned pineapple). Simmer gently to thicken; toss the vegetables with the sauce and serve.

[147]

BAKED SHITAKE [serves 4]

175gm (6oz) fresh Shitake
30gm (1oz) butter
Salt

Remove stems from Shitake. Quarter caps if large and chop stems into small pieces. Place on foil, dot with butter and sprinkle with salt. Wrap round completely with foil and bake in a hot oven, 200°C (Gas Mark 6) for 15–20 minutes. This makes a superb starter and is best served with fresh bread. It reveals the distinctive flavour of Shitake, untainted by anything else.

(with thanks to Bill Slee)

BAKED SEAFOOD WITH SHITAKE [serves 4]

700gm (1½lbs) firm white (cod, haddock or John Dore)
225gm (4oz) prawns
175gm (6oz) Shitake mushrooms
Lemon juice

Sauce
30gm (1oz) butter
30gm (1oz) flour
300ml (½pt) milk
Dash white wine (optional)
60gm (2oz) grated cheese
Salt and pepper

Topping
60gm (2oz) breadcrumbs
30gm (1oz) grated cheese
Finely chopped mushroom stems

Skin fish and cut into 2.5cm (1in) cubes (2.5cm/1in wide strips with smaller fish). Place in buttered, ovenproof dish: pour over milk and bake in oven, 180°C (Gas Mark 4) for about 30 minutes.

Drain milk and juices from fish and use to make sauce adding wine and grated cheese when sauce thickens. Season with salt and pepper to taste.

Remove stems from Shitake mushrooms and set aside for topping. Cut caps into quarters and add to fish with prawns; add a squeeze of lemon juice. Pour sauce over fish and mushroom mixture. Top with breadcrumbs, grated cheese and mushroom stems. Bake for a further 10 minutes at 200°C (Gas Mark 6).

Note: There is infinite scope for varying this recipe.
Any firm fresh fish can be used and any shellfish can be added.

CREAM OF HONEY FUNGUS SOUP   [*serves 3–4*]

225gm (8oz) Honey Fungus finely
chopped
850ml (1½pts) milk
140ml (¼pt) double cream
15ml (1 level tbsp) flour
3 shallots, finely chopped
30gm (1oz) butter
Seasoning

*Melt the butter in a saucepan and stir
in the flour; add the milk, stirring
continually; add the chopped
mushrooms, shallots and seasoning.
Cook gently for 20 minutes, stirring
occasionally. When thickened, remove
from the heat and add the cream.*

COLD MUSHROOM CONSOMMÉ   [*serves 2*]

225gm (8oz) wild mushrooms
300ml (½pt) stock
Cucumber
Seasoning
Lemon

*Process the mushrooms in a liquidiser
and simmer with the stock for 20 minutes.
Strain through a sieve, allow to cool and
add small sliced pieces of cucumber.
Add lemon juice and seasoning to taste.
Refreshing on a warm summer evening.*

WHITE CHAMPIGNON SAUCE

110gm (4oz) dried or fresh Fairy Ring
Champignons
30gm (1oz) butter
30gm (1oz) flour
600ml (1pt) milk

*Simmer the chopped mushrooms in
the milk until tender. Melt the butter
in a saucepan, and carefully mix in the
flour; add the milk and mushrooms slowly,
stirring constantly; season and cook
over a low flame for about 5 minutes.*

STUFFED PUFF BALLS   [*serves 4*]

1 fresh firm white Giant Puff Ball
390gm (14oz) can chestnut stuffing
1 small onion
225gm (8oz) back bacon
Seasoning

*the soft inner part. Chop finely. Peel
and chop the onion. Soften in a little
heated butter or oil. Mix Puff Ball and
onion with the chestnut stuffing,
season to taste and spoon the mixture
into the 'shells' of the Puff Ball. Close
the ball again and drape with bacon
rashers. Wrap in foil and bake in a
pre-heated oven at 170°C (Gas mark
6) for 30 minutes.*

*Clean the Puff Ball well but do not
peel. Slice into 2 halves and scrape out*

SALADE DE FOIE GRAS AUX CÈPES [*serves 4*]

225gm (8oz) fresh Ceps
60gm (2oz) butter
30gm (1oz) chopped shallots
1 small lola rosa
1 small curly endive
1 small raddicio
Walnut Oil/Champagne Vinegar –
3 part oil to 1 part vinegar
4×85gm (3oz) fresh goose liver slices
(you could use cold pâté instead)

Clean and slice Ceps. Pick, wash and drain salad. Mix oil and vinegar together; season with salt, pepper and coriander. Put dressing on salad to taste. Place a little of the salad in the centre of four plates.

Cook shallots in butter without colour, add fresh Ceps. Cook on both sides for two minutes, then arrange around the salad. Cook goose liver in a non-stick pan, for 2 minutes each side, and place on salad.

(*with thanks to David Chambers*)   *fillet of*

FILET DE CHEVREUIL [*serves 4*]

4 potato baskets
300ml (½pt) red wine
1 fillet of venison, weighing between
450 and 900gm (1–2lbs)
335gm (12oz) mixed wild mushrooms
(*Pieds de Mouton*, Chanterelles, Ceps)
225gm (8oz) cleaned button onions
225gm (8oz) mixed baby vegetables –
carrots, Brussel sprouts, corn
1 bunch mixed chopped herbs
600ml (1pt) rich venison sauce made
from the bones
110gm (4oz) mirepoix (carrots, onions,
celery, leek)

Marinade venison in red wine, with vegetables and fresh herbs for 6 hours. Then use marinade to make the brown sauce.

Cut the venison into approximately 12 60gm (2oz) pieces (noisettes).

Cook button onions in boiling, salted water for 3 minutes (refresh in cold water, then colour lightly in butter). Cook vegetables in boiling, salted water, then refresh in cold water. Toss in butter to heat. Cook fillets of venison quickly in a hot non-stick pan with a little oil and butter. Arrange nicely on plate. In the middle, place the potato basket and fill with the baby vegetables. Cook shallots in butter without colour and add wild mushrooms, tossing gently.

In between each noisette of venison place a spoonful of wild mushrooms, top with chopped herbs. Arrange baby onion neatly around the outside, and pour sauce over the dish.

(*with thanks to David Chambers*)

TAGLIATELLI AU RAGOUT DE CHAMPIGNONS SAUVAGES

[*serves 4*]

225gm (8oz) mixed or plain tagliatelli
60gm (2oz) chopped shallots
335gm (12oz) mixed wild mushrooms
2 tomatoes
6 basil leaves
110gm (4oz) butter
300ml (½pt) double cream

Blanch tomatoes in salted, boiling water for 30 seconds; cool quickly in cold water then remove skin; cut in half and take out pips. Cut flesh into 0.5cm (¼in) thick dice.

Cook tagliatelli for 2 minutes in salted, boiling water. Refresh in cold water and wash well to remove stock.

Melt half the butter in a pan, then add shallots and cook without colour; add wild mushrooms, cook for 3 minutes tossing gently. Add double cream and reduce, ('boil down'), till sauce coats a spoon, add shredded basil and diced tomato. Check seasoning.

Warm pasta in remainder of butter. Serve pasta on to four plates and pour on mushroom ragout.

(with thanks to David Chambers)

DIAMANT DE SOLE AU TROMPETTES DE LA MORT [*serves 4*]

8 large fillets of Dover sole cut into diamonds (3 diamonds from each fillet)
450gm (1lb) Trompette mushrooms
225gm (8oz) mussels (cleaned)
110gm (4oz) Horn of Plenty mushrooms (*Pieds de Mouton*)
110gm (4oz) mangetout
600ml (1pt) lobster cream sauce
110gm (4oz) butter
1 bunch chopped chives
60gm (2oz) shallots

Trim and wash Trompette mushrooms. Cook shallots in butter without colour and add trompettes, tossing gently.

Warm mussels, mangetout and Pied de Mouton *mushrooms in a little butter.*

Lightly colour Sole fillet in a non-stick pan for about 1½ minutes each side. When sole is cooked, lay out 6 diamonds on each plate like a star; in between add a spoonful of Trompette mushrooms topped with chives. Take your mixture of mussels, mangetout and Pied de Mouton *and place a spoonful in the centre of each plate. Pour sauce nicely in between fish.*

(with thanks to David Chambers)

WILD MUSHROOM ON TOAST [*serves 4*]

225gm (8oz) moderately flavoured wild
mushrooms, chopped
30ml (2tbsp) flour
15ml (1tbsp) oil
1 onion, finely chopped
1 small red pepper, diced
200gm (7oz) skimmed milk
Seasoning
4 toasted slices wholemeal bread

*Heat oil and soften onion and red
pepper slowly in a covered pan for 5
minutes. Stir in the diced mushrooms
and cook for 3 minutes. Stir in the
flour and cook briefly. Gradually add
the milk and bring to the boil, stirring
constantly. Season to taste. Spoon
over hot toast.*

(with thanks to the Mushroom Growers' Association)

MUSHROOM AND WHEAT TOMATOES [*serves 4*]

75gm (3oz) Bulgar wheat, covered with
cold water and left to soak for 8 hours
225gm (8oz) wild mushrooms, very
finely chopped
30ml (2tbsp) chopped fresh parsley
30ml (2tbsp) lemon juice
15ml (1tbsp) clear honey
Salt and pepper
4 large tomatoes, each weighing 225g
(8oz)

*Drain wheat well, then mix with
remaining ingredients. Cut a thin slice
from the rounded end of each tomato.
Using a small spoon, scoop out the inside
of the tomatoes (reserve to make soups,
sauces etc). Press mushroom mixture into
tomato shells, then chill before serving.*

*To serve hot, place tomatoes in an
ovenproof dish, then bake in oven at
190°C (Gas Mark 5) for about 15 minutes.*

(with thanks to the Mushroom Growers' Association)

MARINADED MUSHROOMS IN GRAPE JUICE [*serves 4–6*]

75gm (3oz) dwarf stick beans, cut into
5cm (2in) lengths
2 apples, cored and thinly sliced
30ml (2 tbsp) lemon juice
450gm (1lb) chopped mushrooms
200ml (7fl oz) white grape juice
50gm (2oz) walnuts, chopped
Salt and pepper

*Cook beans in boiling water for 2
minutes. Plunge into cold water, then
drain well. Mix apples and lemon juice
together. Place mushrooms in a large
bowl with beans, apples and lemon
juice, then stir in remaining
ingredients. Cover and chill for at least
2 hours.*

(with thanks to the Mushroom Growers' Association)

CHILLED MUSHROOM AND HAM SOUP [serves 4–6]

30ml (2tbsp) oil
1 onion, finely chopped
225gm (8oz) wild mushrooms, thinly sliced
30ml (2tbsp) flour
300ml (½pt) vegetable stock or water
Large pinch of celery salt
Large pinch of paprika
Salt and pepper
300ml (½pt) milk
110gm (4oz) lean ham, diced
140ml (5fl oz) carton single cream

To garnish: chopped fresh parsley

Heat oil and cook onion and mushrooms over a gentle heat in a covered pan for 5 minutes, stirring occasionally. Stir in flour and cook a minute. Gradually stir in stock or water. Bring to boil, stirring. Add seasonings and simmer gently for about 3 minutes. Cool, then stir in remaining ingredients. Chill, then serve garnished with parsley.

To serve hot: follow recipe but add stock and milk together. Bring to boil and simmer for 5 minutes. Stir in ham and cream, then heat through, but do not allow soup to boil.

(with thanks to the Mushroom Growers' Association)

GLAZED MUSHROOM FLAN [serves 6–8]

24cm (9½in) cooked pastry flan case
15ml (1tbsp) wholegrain mustard
350gm (12oz) wild mushrooms
60ml (4tbsp) oil
335gm (12oz) carton natural cottage cheese
2 eggs, beaten
15ml (1tbsp) chopped fresh parsley
Salt and freshly milled black pepper
10ml (2tbsp) powdered gelatine
200ml (7fl oz) very hot clear vegetable stock

Spread base of flan case with wholegrain mustard. Slice stalks off mushrooms close to the mushroom caps. Reserve about 20 mushrooms.

Chop remaining mushrooms together with the leftover stalks. Heat oil and cook the whole mushrooms first. Drain well on kitchen paper. Cook remaining chopped mushrooms and drain well.

Scatter the chopped mushrooms over the base of the flan. Beat cheese, eggs, parsley and seasoning together, then turn into flan case. Bake in oven at 180°C (Gas Mark 4) for 30 minutes. Cool. Arrange cooked whole mushrooms on the flan. Sprinkle gelatine over stock, then stir until gelatine has dissolved. When beginning to set, brush glaze over mushrooms. Chill until set.

(with thanks to the Mushroom Growers' Association)

WILD MUSHROOM AND CHICKEN LAYER PIE   [*serves 6*]

30ml (2tbsp) oil
275gm (10oz) wild mushrooms, finely chopped
450gm (1lb) sausagemeat
7.5ml (1½tsp) dried sage
Salt and pepper

Pastry
175gm (6oz) white plain flour
175gm (6oz) malted brown flour
175gm (6oz) margarine
Cold water to mix

225gm (8oz) skinless chicken breast fillet, thinly sliced

To glaze: Beaten egg or milk

Heat oil and cook mushrooms in a covered pan over a medium heat for about 8 minutes, stirring occasionally. Drain well. Mix sausagemeat, sage, seasoning and mushrooms together. Mix flours together, then rub in margarine. Stir in enough water to form a not too stiff dough. Roll ⅔ pastry out thinly and use to line a 1.1 litre (2pt) pie dish. Place half the sausagemeat in the bottom, followed by a layer of chicken, and then topped with remaining sausagemeat. Roll out remaining pastry and use to cover pie, sealing edges well. Decorate with pastry leaves cut from trimmings. Brush with egg or milk. Bake in oven at 190°C (Gas Mark 5) for about 1 hour, covering with aluminium foil if necessary. Serve hot or cold.

(*with thanks to the Mushroom Growers' Association*)

MELZER'S IODINE REAGENT (see page 49)

1.5gm Iodine crystals
5gm Potassium iodide
100gm Chloral hydrate
100ml distilled or deionised water

Add the ingredients together and heat gently until dissolved.

Positive amyloid reaction: colour changes to black when applied to spores thickly grouped on slide.

Positive dextrinoid reaction: colour changes to rust when applied to spores thickly grouped on slide.

GLOSSARY OF TERMS

agaric	gill-bearing fungus (see p. 46)
alkaloid	complex nitrogen-containing toxin
Ascomycete	fungus shedding ascospores from ascus (see p. 48)
ascus	spore-containing flask
autodigestion	release of spores by decomposition
basal bulb	swollen base of stem
Basidiomycete	fungus shedding basidiospores
basidium	spore generating hyphal tip
bracket	familiar name for plate-like fungi on trees
button	immature unopened sporophore
cap	upper part of agaric sporophore
decurrent	describing gill outline (see p. 24)
flush	appearance of a crop of mushrooms
gill	vertical plate bearing spores
gleba	spore-mass of puffball (see p. 47)
hymenium	spore-producing layer of mycelium
hypha	individual thread of fungal tissue
metabolism	life-process of fungus
mushroom	popular name for familiar edible fungus
mycelium	cotton-wool-like mass of hyphae
mycorrhiza	host plant root associated with fungus
parasite	fungus on living host
pileus	cap covering gills or pores (see p. 46)
pore	external opening of hymenial tube
ring	remains of veil on stem
saprophyte	fungus on dead or dying host
sclerotium	fruiting body of *Claviceps* etc.
sinuate	describing gill outline (see p. 24)
spawn	commercial mycelium inoculate
spore	'seed' of fungus
sporophore	fruiting part of fungus
thermolabile	chemical destroyed by heat
toadstool	unfamiliar or inedible fungus
toxin	poisonous chemical substance
truffle	type of subterranean fruiting body

umbo	hump or boss on cap
veil	protective covering for gills (young)
vernal	spring appearance
volva	sheath at base of stalk

BIBLIOGRAPHY

Badham C. D. *Esculent Funguses of England* London 1863

Barger G. *Ergot and Ergotism* Gurney and Jackson 1931

Buller A. H. R. *The Fungus Lore of Greeks and Romans* London 1915

Carluccio, Antonio *A Passion for Mushrooms* Pavilion 1989

Dearness J. *The Personal Factor in Mushroom Poisoning* Mycologia 3. 1911

Findlay W.P.K. *Fungi: Folklore Fiction and Fact* Kingsprint 1982

Ford W. W. *The Pathology of Amanita phalloides intoxication* Journal of Infectious Diseases. 5 (pp 115–133) 1908

Grigson, Jane *The Mushroom Feast* Penguin 1987

Hartley D. M. *Food in England* MacDonalds 1954

Houghton W. *Notices of Fungi in Greek and Latin Authors* Annals and Magazine of Natural History Ser. 5:5 (pp 22–49) 1885

Jochelson W. *Religion and Myths of the Koryak in Jesup North Pacific Expedition* Mems. Am. Nat. Hist. Soc. 1906

Jordan M. *A Guide to Mushrooms* Millington 1975

Lange M. and Bayard Hora F. *Mushrooms and Toadstools* Collins 1963

Lucas E. H. *Folklore and Plant Drugs* Michigan Academy of Science Arts and Letters 45 (pp 127–136) 1960

Phillips R. *Mushrooms and Other Fungi of Great Britain and Europe* Pan Books 1981

USEFUL ADDRESSES

For details of how to join the British Mycological Society, write to them:
c/o C.A.B. International Mycological Institute,
Ferry Lane, Kew, Surrey, TW9 3AF.

The society's journal, *The Mycologist*, is free to members
but also available by subscription from:
Journals Subscription Manager, Cambridge University Press,
The Edinburgh Building, Shaftesbury Road, Cambridge, CB2 2RU.

The Truffle Festival in Alba takes place in September/October each year.
For exact dates contact: Italian Tourist Office, 1 Princes St., London W1.
Tel: 01 408 1254

For travel information on the French mushroom/truffle areas contact:
Air France, 158 New Bond St., London W1. Tel: 01 499 9511

SNCF (French Railways Ltd.) 179 Piccadilly, London W1. Tel: 01 409 3518

Do-it-yourself Mushroom Kits are available from most good garden centres or
contact: Mr. A. Focardi, Harper Mushrooms, Four Winds, Kington Lane,
Claverdon, Warwickshire CV35 8PP. Tel: 0926 842093

For details of other cultivated mushroom spores/kits contact:
Samuel Dobie & Sons Ltd, Broomhill Way, Torquay, Devon. TQ2 7QW.
Tel: 0803 616281

Index

Numerals in *italics* refer to captions

A final warning: Never eat any form of fungus unless you are absolutely sure of its identification and safety.